What People Are Saying About

I also bought both the Chakra Healing and Aura Healing DVDs off Steve Murray's website at a special price. If you are looking for a process and method to heal the Chakras and/or Aura this is it. Steve shows you how to heal your own Chakras and Aura and how to heal another person's Chakras and Aura in a step by step format. I recommend both DVDs. *P.R.*

Chakra Healing Step By Step by Reiki Master Steve Murray DVD. A great way to bring this much needed skill into your life. Steve Murray brings a slightly intimidating subject down to earth with easy to follow techniques, careful gentle instruction. The production is well done. *M.W.*

I have other DVDs and books by Steve Murray and I am always happy with his programs. I bought both of his new DVDs Chakra Healing Step by Step and Aura Healing Step by Step off his web site and both are great tutorials for Healing the Chakras and Aura. I highly recommend both if you are interested in learning how to heal the Chakras and Aura. *W.M.*

Reiki 1st Level Attunement Become a Reiki Healer DVD. I paid 2 thousand dollars for my first Reiki Attunement, I felt nothing and could do nothing. I purchased this Dvd on a whim and a desire to help others and wow what a difference and for a mere fraction of the cost of my first attunement. Great work. *S.W.*

Steve Murray's approach to Reiki and healing is excellent. Steve believes that everyone can benefit from Reiki and his materials show you why. He explains the Attunements so you know what you will be doing. The Attunements can be taken over and over, and provide a variety of experiences for the receiver - all positive, in my experience. Steve Murray is a big part of my healing library. *M.N.*

1

This video is a great and affordable way to get your 1st attunement My mother so wanted to get her Reiki, but couldn't afford a class. I'm a Reiki II, so I couldn't pass on the attunement yet, although I can teach her how to be a Reiki I. This is a great teaching tool. *L.L*

THIS PROGRAM WORKS, PERIOD. I did the attunement and can honestly say I am functioning more efficiently, my thinking is much clearer, my intuition of what is correct action is sharper and the attunement produced a great sense of peace. *F.C.*

Steve's set of books and and DVDs that go along with his Reiki Master program are invaluable for the Reiki Practitioner. The Reiki Master Attunement DVD gave me a true attunement, enhancing my healing abilities. Steve's books, Reiki the Ultimate Guides 1, 2, 3, 4 and Reiki Beliefs Exposed For All are fabulous and filled with a wealth of information. His DVD, A Reiki 1st, Aura and Chakra Attunement Performed, is an excellent companion to the books demonstrating the actual processes of performing attunements. I will use this set again and again as reference along my path of Reiki healing. *S.G.*

I have had the pleasure of obtaining Steve Murray's latest masterpiece: Animal Psychic Communication Plus Reiki Pet Healing book. It is truly impressive, the simplicity of his approach makes it one of the most unique and "doable" techniques you will find on this topic. *J.L.*

It's a shame if this amazing healing technique has been kept from anyone because of the cost of classes. Raising the consciousness of this planet should be everyone's priority and learning Reiki is one way we can effect a massive shift for many. My blessings go out to Steve for being a true maverick in this field and letting spirit lead him. *J.G.*

Learn Chakra and Aura Healing
Become a Chakra/Aura Healer

Steve Murray

First Printing

Steve Murray Inc.

Learn Chakra and Aura Healing
Become a Chakra/Aura Healer

Published by
Steve Murray Inc.
9429 Cedar Heights, Las Vegas, NV 89134
Website: www.healingreiki.com
Email: bodymindheal@aol.com

First Printing January 2012

Library of Congress Cataloging-in-Publication Data
Learn Chakra and Aura Healing Become a Chakra/ Aura Healer
/ Murray, Steve – 1st ed.
Library of Congress Control Number: 2011919263
ISBN # 978-0-9828370-2-3

Includes bibliographical references and index.
1. Chakra 2. Auras 3. Chakras 4. Aura 5. Aura Healing 6. Chakra
Healing 7. Spiritual Healing
Cover design: Edyta Sokolowska
Photos: Edyta Sokolowska
Type design, production: Edyta Sokolowska
Editor: Carol von Raesfeld

Printed in the U.SA.

To contact Steve Murray and/or review his Books, DVDS, CDs and Free Offers, visit his web site at www.healingreiki.com

Books By Steve Murray

Animal Psychic Communication Plus Reiki Pet Healing

Reiki The Ultimate Guide Learn Sacred Symbols & Attunements plus Reiki Secrets You Should Know

Reiki The Ultimate Guide, Vol. 2 Learn Reiki Healing with Chakras, plus New Reiki Healing Attunements for All Levels

Reiki the Ultimate Guide, Vol. 3: Learn New Reiki Aura Attunements Heal Mental & Emotional Issues

Reiki The Ultimate Guide Vol. 4 Past Lives & Soul Retrieval Remove Psychic Debris & Heal Your Life

Reiki the Ultimate Guide Vol. 5 Learn New Psychic Attunements to Expand Psychic Gifts & Healing

Reiki False Beliefs Exposed For All Misinformation Kept Secret By a Few Revealed

Cancer Guided Imagery Program for Radiation, Chemotherapy, Surgery and Recovery

Stop Eating Junk Food! In 5 Minutes a Day For 21 Days Let Your Unconscious Mind Do the Work

DVDs By Steve Murray

Chakra Healing Step By Step

Aura Healing Step By Step

Increase Your Psychic Abilities with Contemporary Technology

Increase Your Healing Abilities a Program for all Healers Including Reiki

Reiki Psychic Attunement Open and Expand Your Psychic Abilities

DVDs continued...

Reiki Psychic Attunement Vol. 2 New Attunements
to Expand Psychic Abilities

Remove Psychic Debris & Heal Vol. 1
Access a Past Life With or Without Reiki

Remove Psychic Debris & Heal Vol. 2
Soul Retrieval With or Without Reiki

Remove Psychic Debris & Heal Vol. 3
Detach Negative Psychic Cords With or Without Reiki

Lose Weight Easily with Contemporary Technology
Let your Sub-Mind do the work

Energy Pet Healing Step By Step

Psychic Communication with Pets Step By Step

Reiki: What It Is, How It Heals

Reiki 1st Level Attunement Become a Reiki Healer

Reiki 2nd Level Attunement Learn and Use the Reiki Sacred Symbols

Reiki Master Attunement Become a Reiki Master

Reiki Healing Attunement Heal Emotional-Mental-Physical-Spiritual Issues

A Reiki 1st, Aura and Chakra Attunement Performed

A Reiki Prosperity Attunements to Increase Your Prosperity

Rider-Waite Learning To Read The Tarot Intuitively

Rider-Waite Learning to Read the Symbolism of the Tarot

How To Contact Angels and Departed Love Ones A Step By Step Guide

DVDs continued...

How to Contact Spirits Vol. 2 Learn to use a Spirit/Ouija Board & Hold a Séance

30-Day Subliminal Weight Loss Program: Lose Fat While Your Unconscious Mind Does The Work

Lose Fat and Weight! Stop Eating Junk Food In 5 Minutes a Day For 21 Days

Successfully Preparing For Cancer Chemotherapy Using Your Subconscious Mind

Destroying Cancer Cells Using Your Subconscious Mind

Successfully Preparing For Cancer Radiation Using Your Subconscious Mind

Cancer Guided Imagery Program for Cancer Surgery

Cancer Guided Imagery for Cancer Radiation

Cancer Guided Imagery Program for Cancer Chemotherapy

Cancer Guided Imagery Program for Cancer Recovery

Cancer Guided Imagery Program Destroying Cancer Cells

Pain Relief Using Your Unconscious Mind A Subliminal Program

Fear and Stress Relief Using Your Unconscious Mind A Subliminal Program

Stop Smoking Using Your Unconscious Mind A Subliminal Program

Mind Fitness Workout- Program the Mind for Weight Loss as you Exercise: Walking Workout!

Mind Fitness Workout- Program the Mind for Weight Loss as you Exercise: Dance Workout!

Mind Fitness Workout - Program the Mind for Weight Loss as you
Exercise: Fitness Workout

CDs By Steve Murray

Reiki Healing Music Attunement Volume 1

Reiki Healing Music Attunement Volume 2

Reiki Chakra Music Attunement

Reiki Aura Music Attunement

Reiki Psychic Music Attunement CD Volume I

Reiki Psychic Music Attunement Cd Volume II

Grounding & Clearing Vol. 1 Music with Contemporary Technology for
Healing & Meditation

Grounding & Clearing Vol. 2 Music with Contemporary Technology for
Healing & Meditation

Grounding & Clearing Vol. 1 Music with Contemporary Technology for
Healing & Meditation

Disclaimer

The information presented in this book is intended for people interested in the Aura and Chakra. What is taught in the book and in the video is not intended to be a substitute for medical treatment. The healing methods taught in all of Steve Murray's books, CDs, and DVDs should never be considered a sole method of treatment for any illness or disease. *Never stop your medical treatment for any illness or disease without first consulting with your doctor.*

This book is dedicated to

All the Current Chakra/Aura Healers
and
Future Chakra /Aura Healers

CONTENTS

Chapter 1 Introduction   13

Chakra Segment

Chapter 2 Universal Life Force   17
Chapter 3 Purpose of a Chakra Healing   31
Chapter 4 Areas of Influence   35
Chapter 5 Selecting the Chakra For Healing   41
Chapter 6 Chakra Healing Step By Step   53
Chapter 7 Two Chakra Healing Examples   61
Chapter 8 Chakra Points to Remember   103

Aura Segment

Chapter 9 Aura Defined   109
Chapter 10 Aura Layers   113
Chapter 11 Purpose of an Aura Healing   131
Chapter 12 Aura Healing Step By Step   137
Chapter 13 Two Aura Healing Examples   149
Chapter 14 Seeing Auras   179
Chapter 15 Aura Points to Remember   195
Chapter 16 Aura Protection   201

Additional Information

Index   203
Selected Bibliography   204
Information on Chakra/Aura Healer Certification   207
Steve Murray Bio   208

Movement is a medicine for creating change in a person's physical, emotional, and mental states.

-Carol Welchm

Introduction

You are about to embark on a journey where you will learn how to perform two powerful, but easy to learn healing methods. One method will be Chakra Healing. Chakra Healing is performed to help heal ailments or disease in the physical body.

The second method is Aura Healing. Aura Healing is performed for mental, emotional, and spiritual issues. By learning and becoming proficient at these two healing modalities, you will become a Chakra/Aura Healer. Thus, you will be able to help heal physical challenges and/or mental and emotional issues on yourself and others.

Any person can learn how to perform my Chakra and Aura Healing methods. You do not need to be a trained Healer. If you are now a Healer, you can incorporate both the Chakra and the Aura Healing into the healing modality you are now using, such as Reiki. Although this is a standalone book with regard to learning Chakra and Aura Healing, I have two DVDs available — "Learn Chakra Healing Step By Step" and "Learn Aura Healing Step By Step" — that together with this book are the basis for my Chakra/Aura Healer certification program. If you wish to be certified as a Chakra/Aura Healer, information is available at my website: www.healingreiki.com.

The book is divided into two segments. The first segment explains the Chakras and my method for Chakra Healing. The second segment explains the Aura and my method for Aura Healing.

Okay, let's get started on your healing journey to become a Chakra/Aura Healer.

Chakra Segment

The body never lies.
  - Martha Graham

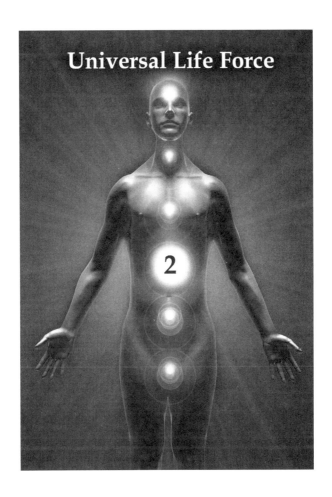

Universal Life Force

We are alive because a Universal Life Force flows through our physical body, nourishing every single cell and supporting all organs. When the flow of this Life Force is disrupted, illness or disease can manifest.

When this flow stops, the physical body dies. This Universal Life force has many names in different cultures. A few examples are "Chi," "Mana," "Ki," "Holy Spirit," and "Reiki." Throughout this book I will refer to the Universal Life Force as "Life Force."

The source of the Life Force is not within us; it originates outside of us and also has many names such as "Higher Power," "Higher Dimension," "God," etc. There are many theories and beliefs that explain the Life Force and its source, but the fact is, no one in the physical world really can prove which one is correct.

The Life Force flows into the body through non-physical energy portals that are located on the surface of the body. These portals are called "Chakras." Chakra is a Sanskrit word meaning "spinning wheel" or "vortex." The spinning motion of the Chakra forms a cavity or vacuum in the center of it, drawing the Life Force into the body. Once the Chakra takes the Life Force into the body, it also acts as a pump or valve, regulating the flow of the Life Force throughout the body so it can be used as needed.

People who can see Chakras describe them as being about the size of your fist and when looking directly at them, they resemble a spinning wheel. A Chakra is cone-shaped with its opening (vortex) extending about four to six inches away from your body. The Chakra vortex is tight and compact near the surface of the skin, gradually widening as it extends outside the physical body.

Seven Major Chakras

There are Seven Major Chakras (Reference Illus. 1). The following are the locations of the Seven Major Chakras and the color commonly associated with each Chakra when it is healthy.

- The 1st Chakra is also known as the "Root Chakra" or "Base Chakra." It is located at the base of the spine. Its color is red.

- The 2nd Chakra is also known as the "Sacral Chakra" or "Sexual Chakra." It is located just beneath the navel. Its color is orange.

- The 3rd Chakra is also known as the "Solar Plexus Chakra." It is located at the base of the sternum. The common color linked to this Chakra is yellow, although the colors green and pink in the next Chakra are also sometimes associated with it.

- The 4th Chakra is also known as the "Heart Chakra." It is located in the area near the heart. This chakra has two colors associated with it — green and pink.

- The 5th Chakra is also known as the "Throat Chakra." It is located in the throat. Its color is blue.

- The 6th Chakra is also known as the "Brow Chakra" or "Third Eye." It is located a little above the area between the eyebrows. Its color is purple.

7 Major Chakras

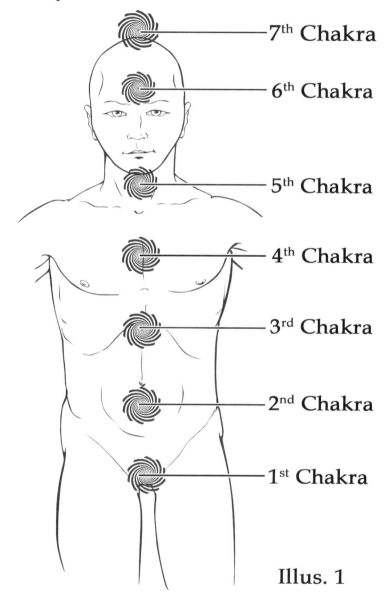

7th Chakra

6th Chakra

5th Chakra

4th Chakra

3rd Chakra

2nd Chakra

1st Chakra

Illus. 1

- 7th Chakra is also known as the "Crown Chakra." It is located on top of the head. This Chakra is commonly believed to be where the soul enters the physical body at birth and from which it departs at the time of death. Three colors most frequently associated with this Chakra are white, violet, and gold.

The Six Major Chakras on the front side of the physical body, (not the 7th Chakra) also have a corresponding Back Chakra (Illus. 2) that is aligned and connected to an energy channel that is behind and parallel with the Chakras on the front side of the body (Illus. 3). Notice on Illus. 3 that some front Chakras are deeper than others in the body and the back Chakras are not deep at all.

The 7th Major Chakra is directly on top of the head. It is said that it does have a back Chakra, but it is located where all dimensions become one.

With my Chakra healing method you will work with both sides of the Chakra, except the 7th Chakra. The reason I have you work with Back Chakras is simple. If one side of the Chakra is unhealthy, then the other side can become unhealthy, if is not already. Usually back Chakras are neglected in Chakra Healing because the majority of Chakra teachings focus on the Chakras on the front side of the body. Information that is available on the Back Chakras is sometimes confusing and conflicting, to say the least. All you really need to know about the Back Chakras for my Chakra Healing method is this:

The 6 Major Back Chakras

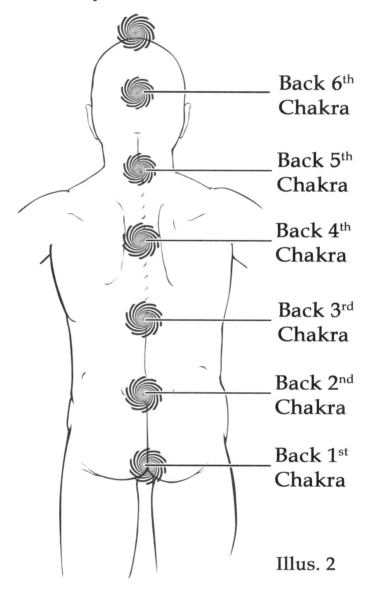

Back 6th Chakra

Back 5th Chakra

Back 4th Chakra

Back 3rd Chakra

Back 2nd Chakra

Back 1st Chakra

Illus. 2

Chakras Front & Back Vortexes

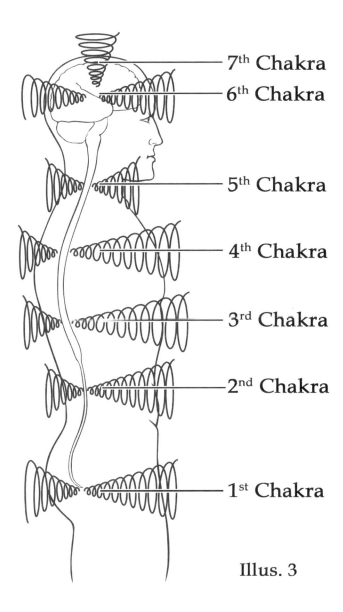

7th Chakra

6th Chakra

5th Chakra

4th Chakra

3rd Chakra

2nd Chakra

1st Chakra

Illus. 3

• The locations of the Back Chakras which I will supply.
• Each Back Chakra correlates with the same body systems and body organs as its corresponding Front Chakra.
• The front side of the Major Chakras corresponds to our conscious, physical being and the laws of the physical universe.
• The back side of the Major Chakras correspond to our unconscious, non-physical being and to the laws of the non-physical universe.

Each Chakra spins at a different speed, the slowest is the 1st Chakra and increases as you move up, with the 7th Chakra being the fastest.

Chakras spin in a clockwise direction when you face them. This spinning creates a vibration that resonates as a color and can be seen by some people. The spin speed and vibration of a Chakra is also determined by its health. A Chakra that is not healthy might have a slower spin and a different color.

There are Minor Chakras which are also called "Secondary Chakras" throughout the body. The Major Chakras manage our most critical functions; the Secondary Chakras regulate less fundamental needs. Although you will not be working directly with the Minor Chakras, you should be aware that they exist. The Minor Chakras assist the Major Chakras with their functions. The Minor Chakras are much smaller, vary in size, and are attached to joints, glands, the palms, feet, and nerve clusters throughout the body.

Blocked and Balanced Chakra

A "blocked Chakra" is a general term used to describe a Chakra that is not healthy. A blocked Chakra can be spinning too slowly or spinning in the wrong direction. This can prevent or slow down the Life Force from flowing into it. If there is a block in a Chakra, most of the time there is an illness or disease in its Area of Influence. (I will explain this in the next chapter.) If a Chakra's block is not cleared, there can be a domino effect on the other Chakras. This can compound any physical illness that has already manifested and may create more physical problems.

The term "balanced Chakra" refers to a Chakra that has healthy spin and color with the Life Force flowing into it without a problem. The good news is if you have a blocked Chakra, most of the time it can be returned to a balanced state with a Chakra Healing.

Meridians

Chakras send Life Force throughout the body though pathways or energy channels called "Meridians." Meridians are the equivalent of our blood vessels throughout the body, but instead of transporting blood, they transport your Life Force.

There are two systems of Meridians that form a network of energy channels throughout the body: Major Meridians and Secondary Meridians. There are twelve Major Meridians and hundreds of Secondary Meridians.

The twelve Major Meridians run up and down the body (Illus. 4 and 5) and are interconnected with the Major Chakras and pass through internal organs. The Secondary Meridians are connected to the Major Meridians and are spread throughout the rest of the body.

Different Chakra Teachings

There are conflicting teachings with Chakras. They all are correct within the healing modalities in which they are taught. If you discover your previous knowledge of Chakras differs from mine on one or more points, do not worry about it. This will not matter with the Chakra Healing method I will show you. Here are a few examples of different Chakra teachings:

- The Chakras' spin direction is counter-clockwise
- Back Chakras are not mentioned
- Locations and functions of the Minor Chakras
- Additional Major Chakras
- Names of the Seven Major Chakras
- Colors of the Chakras are different
- Meridians are called "Nadis"

Major Front Meridians

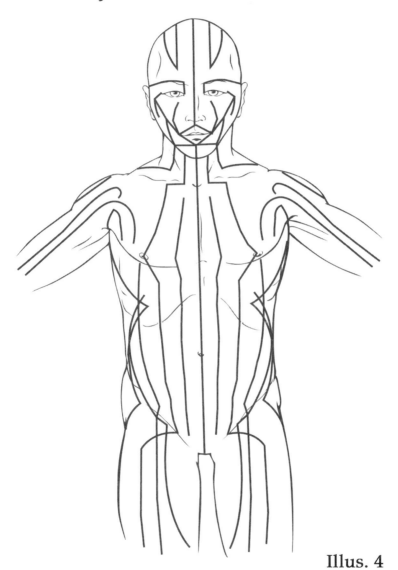

Illus. 4

Major Back Meridians

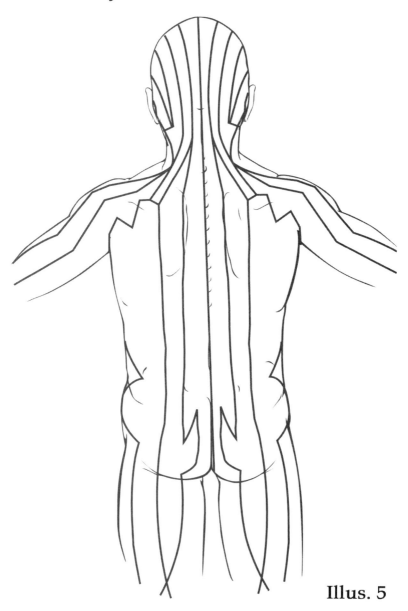

Illus. 5

The best and most efficient pharmacy is within your own system.

- Robert C. Peale

Chakras are energy-awareness centers. They are the revolving doors of creativity and communication between spirit and the world.

- Michael J. Tamura

Purpose of a Chakra Healing

3

When a person has a physical health issue, their life energy is usually stretched thin and depleted from the health issue. The purpose of a Chakra Healing session is to send Life Force directly into the Chakra that is responsible for the Area of Influence in which the health issue has manifested and/or is located. Once this is done, the Life Force is processed by the Chakra to help the health issue and what Life Force is left, if any, moves through the rest of the Chakra System.

The metaphor for this method of Chakra Healing is you are a powerful battery charger of Life Force and you will give a charge of the Life Force to yourself or others whose Life Force is low because of a health issue. This will supply additional Life Force to continue to help heal any health challenge in the physical body, but you must make sure the battery charger is connected to the correct place in the body to be effective. You will learn the correct place to connect it in my Chakra Healing steps.

Life Force is very powerful, but it is a very subtle force when it flows into a Chakra. If Life Force was like a charge of electricity, there would be major problems with your body accepting and utilizing it. Once you are experienced at performing Chakra Healing, you will be able to sense the flow of Life Force as you send it during the Healing session.

Chakra Sensations

Every person will have their own unique experience during a Chakra Healing. You should be aware of some of the possibilities so there will be no fear or surprises if giving one to yourself or another person. Here are a few examples of what can be experienced during a healing:

- A Chakra feeling warm or hot
- A rushing sensation going into a Chakra
- A Chakra feels like it is spinning
- A flow of energy throughout the body
- The body feeling warm or hot
- Feeling totally relaxed

A person might have an emotional release that can include crying or a runny nose during or right after a Chakra Healing. This is part of the healing process. It is harmless and always temporary. Or, maybe nothing at all will be experienced consciously during a Chakra Healing. If this happens, it does not mean the Chakra Healing has not been successful. The results will be the same, with or without physical sensations, if the Chakra Healing is performed correctly.

Put your future in good hands - your own.
                                    - Author Unknown

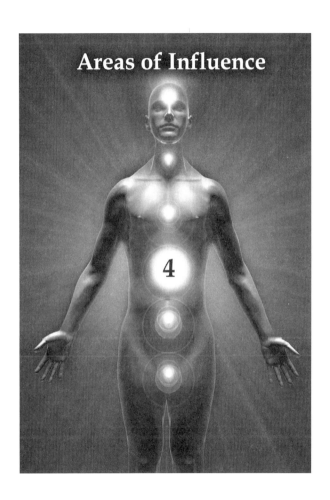

Each Major Chakra, front and back, has an Area of Influence. The knowledge of each Chakra's Area of Influence is an important element in Chakra Healing. The Chakra's Area of Influence is determined by its location and surrounding area where it is located.

In this Area of Influence each Chakra is responsible for maintaining the health of a specific organ, body parts (such as legs and arms), glands, and nerves. In addition, certain Chakras are responsible for maintaining the health of the physical body's internal systems. The internal systems are:

• **Muscular System**
Muscles make up half of the body's systems. These include voluntary muscles to lift objects, move, etc., and involuntary muscles, which include heart muscle and smooth muscle to provide power for the Digestive, Cardiovascular, and Respiratory Systems.

• **Skeletal System**
The skeletal system is the structure, bones on which the body is built. It is the body's foundation.

• **Nervous System**
The brain is the site of conscious and unconscious thought. Through the nerves of the spinal cord and the nerves that spread throughout the body, the brain controls all body movement and function.

• **Endocrine System**
The endocrine system plays a major role in the body's daily health. The glands release hormones directly into the bloodstream and control all aspects of growth, development, and daily bodily functions.

• **Reproductive System**
The gonads, the primary reproductive organs, are the testes in the male and the ovaries in the female. These

organs are responsible for producing the sperm and ova, but they secrete hormones and are also considered endocrine glands.

• Urinary System
This system's primary function is the kidneys' production of urine to eliminate waste and excess fluids.

• Digestive System
The digestive system starts at the mouth and ends at the anus. The system has many functions, but the main ones are storing food, digesting it, and eliminating waste.

• Respiratory System
The respiratory system carries air in and out of the lungs where oxygen and carbon dioxide are exchanged.

• Cardiovascular System
This system's main purpose is to pump oxygenated blood throughout the body. Blood circulation also removes waste products from the body.

• Lymphatic / Immune System
The lymphatic system functions include the transport of lymphatic fluid, which can carry bacteria and cancer cells. Lymph glands are found throughout the body and swell up when infected to prevent the spread of disease and infections. The lymphatic system is a major element in our physical body's defense system.

Here is more information on the glands in the Endocrine System that I feel you should know. When you understand what they do within the body, you will see why it is vital to your wellbeing that they are healthy.

• **Gonads**
Gonads secrete hormones that affect all aspects of sexuality in men and women throughout their lives. This includes reproduction, puberty, fertility, menstruation, pregnancy, menopause, sex drive, etc.

• **Pancreas**
The pancreas secretes two major hormones, insulin and glucagon. The human body needs blood glucose (blood sugar) balanced. Insulin and glucagon are the hormones that do this. Glucose is the only food substance utilized by the brain.

• **Adrenal Glands**
The Adrenal Glands have two separate parts — the medulla and the cortex. The medulla secretes adrenaline which acts directly on the heart, blood vessels, lungs, and muscles in the "fight or flight" response. The cortex secretes steroids, which balances the physical and emotional levels. This helps with shock and stress.

It also produces Aldosterone which balances water, sodium, and potassium. This helps maintain normal blood pressure.

• **Thymus**
Although all the functions of the Thymus are not fully understood, we do know it is important to the body's immune response, especially the production of T-cells.

Auto-immune diseases, including AIDS, are affected by the thymus, as are some forms of cancer.

• Thyroid and Parathyroid

The Thyroid gland affects metabolism in several ways growth, temperature control, energy production, and carbohydrate and fat metabolism. The Parathyroid consists of four glands that are vital to calcium metabolism which is needed for healthy teeth, bones, and muscles, including the heart.

• Pituitary and Hypothalamus

The Pituitary gland regulates the entire endocrine system. The Hypothalamus secretes hormones which, in turn, regulate the flow of hormones from the Pituitary. The Hypothalamus gland also directs the body's thirst, hunger, sexual desire, and the biological clock that determines our aging process.

• Pineal

The pineal gland secretes melatonin which stimulates sleep and controls our body clock and our daily biological rhythms. The area where this gland is located is considered the connecting link between the physical and spiritual worlds.

What lies behind us and what lies before us are tiny matters compared to what lies within us.

- Henry S. Haskins

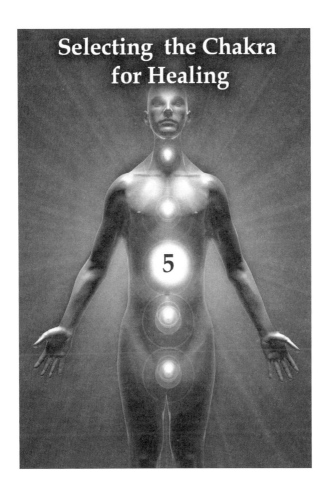

Selecting the Chakra
for Healing

Before performing a Chakra Healing on yourself or another person, you must identify the specific physical ailment or disease for which the Chakra Healing is to be performed. You also need to know where that ailment or disease has manifested in the body.

This information is usually obtained from a medical diagnosis and/or asking your doctor. Once you have the knowledge where the ailment or disease has manifested in the body, use the following illustrations and guidelines to decide which Chakra to use during a Chakra Healing.

Seven Illustrations

There are seven illustrations at the end of this chapter to help determine which Chakra you will use in a Chakra Healing. Each illustration shows the Seven Major Chakras with the surrounding organs, glands, nerves, etc. located in their Area of Influence.

Guidelines For Using The Illustrations

Review the illustrations and find the one that shows the organ, body part, body system, etc., where the ailment or disease has manifested for the Chakra Healing you will be doing. Then look at the Chakra's Area of Influence in which the organ, body part, body system, etc. is located. That's the Chakra you will use during a Chakra Healing.

For example, the Chakra Healing is for a kidney infection. Look at the illustration that shows the kidneys, then see which Chakra's Area of Influence the kidneys are in and that's the Chakra you will use during the Chakra Healing. In this example, you would use Illustration 4 and you would discover the kidneys are in the 3rd Chakra's Area of Influence. If the area where the ailment or disease is located overlaps two Chakras' Areas of Influence, you should use the Chakra that has the largest Area of Influence.

On occasion, the illustrations might not show the organ, gland, body part, body system, etc. that was diagnosed as the problem. If that happens, all you need to know is the location or the body system it is in. To get this information you can either ask the doctor or do research; then look for the area on an illustration to see in which Chakra's Area of Influence it is located and that is the Chakra you will use during the Healing.

The majority of the time you will use the illustrations to determine the Chakra to use for a Chakra Healing. However, a physical ailment or disease sometimes is not localized, but is manifested throughout a body system. When this happens, use the next guidelines to determine which Chakra to use.

- For ailments or diseases within the lower body, legs and feet, use the 1st Chakra.
- For ailments or diseases of the skin, use the 2nd Chakra.
- For ailments or diseases that are blood specific, use the 3rd Chakra.
- For ailments or diseases that are in the Lymphatic/Immune system, use the 4th Chakra.
- For ailments or diseases that are in the circulatory system, use the 4th Chakra.
- For ailments or diseases within the shoulders, arms, and hands, use the 4th Chakra.
- For colds, flus, or viruses, use the 5th Chakra.
- For ailments or diseases that are in the autonomic nervous system, use the 6th Chakra.

- For ailments or diseases that are in the central nervous system, use the 7th Chakra.
- For ailments or diseases that are in the Skeletal System or Muscular System, use the 7th Chakra.

Skeletal / Muscular System

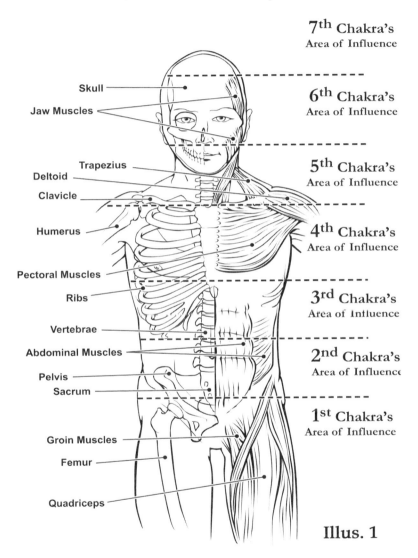

7th Chakra's
Area of Influence

Skull

Jaw Muscles

6th Chakra's
Area of Influence

Trapezius

Deltoid

Clavicle

5th Chakra's
Area of Influence

Humerus

4th Chakra's
Area of Influence

Pectoral Muscles

Ribs

3rd Chakra's
Area of Influence

Vertebrae

Abdominal Muscles

Pelvis

Sacrum

2nd Chakra's
Area of Influence

1st Chakra's
Area of Influence

Groin Muscles

Femur

Quadriceps

Illus. 1

Nervous System

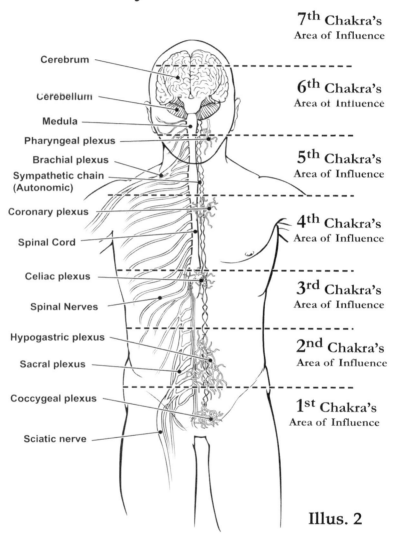

7th Chakra's Area of Influence

Cerebrum

6th Chakra's Area of Influence

Cerebellum

Medula

Pharyngeal plexus

5th Chakra's Area of Influence

Brachial plexus

Sympathetic chain (Autonomic)

Coronary plexus

4th Chakra's Area of Influence

Spinal Cord

Celiac plexus

3rd Chakra's Area of Influence

Spinal Nerves

Hypogastric plexus

2nd Chakra's Area of Influence

Sacral plexus

Coccygeal plexus

1st Chakra's Area of Influence

Sciatic nerve

Illus. 2

Endocrine System

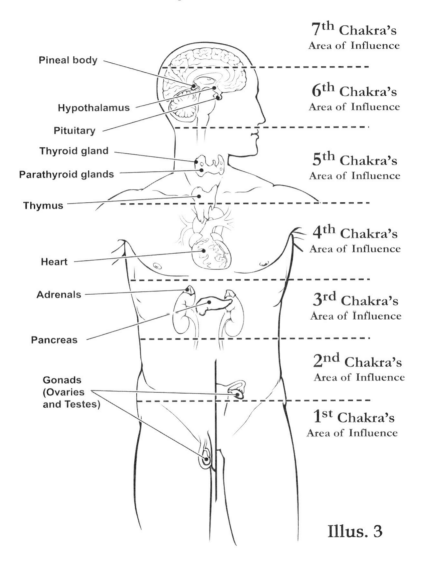

Pineal body

Hypothalamus

Pituitary

Thyroid gland

Parathyroid glands

Thymus

Heart

Adrenals

Pancreas

Gonads
(Ovaries
and Testes)

7th Chakra's
Area of Influence

6th Chakra's
Area of Influence

5th Chakra's
Area of Influence

4th Chakra's
Area of Influence

3rd Chakra's
Area of Influence

2nd Chakra's
Area of Influence

1st Chakra's
Area of Influence

Illus. 3

Reproductive / Urinary System

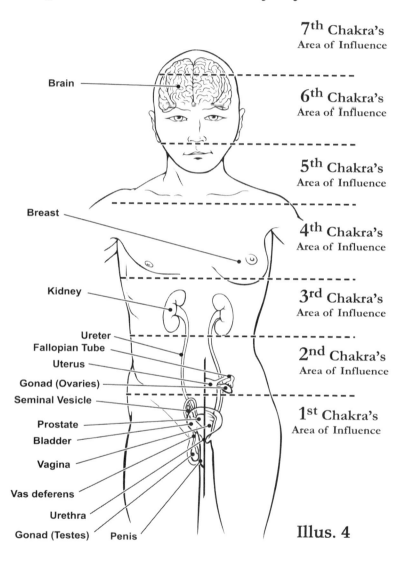

7th Chakra's Area of Influence

Brain

6th Chakra's Area of Influence

5th Chakra's Area of Influence

Breast

4th Chakra's Area of Influence

Kidney

3rd Chakra's Area of Influence

Ureter
Fallopian Tube
Uterus
Gonad (Ovaries)
Seminal Vesicle

2nd Chakra's Area of Influence

Prostate
Bladder
Vagina
Vas deferens
Urethra
Gonad (Testes)   Penis

1st Chakra's Area of Influence

Illus. 4

Digestion System

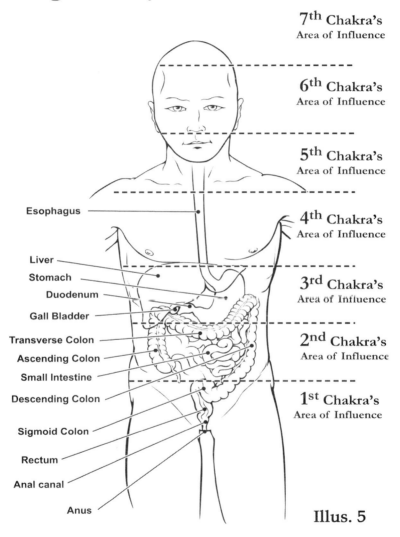

7th Chakra's
Area of Influence

6th Chakra's
Area of Influence

5th Chakra's
Area of Influence

Esophagus

4th Chakra's
Area of Influence

Liver
Stomach
Duodenum

3rd Chakra's
Area of Influence

Gall Bladder

Transverse Colon
Ascending Colon
Small Intestine

2nd Chakra's
Area of Influence

Descending Colon

1st Chakra's
Area of Influence

Sigmoid Colon

Rectum

Anal canal

Anus

Illus. 5

Cardiovascular / Respiratory System

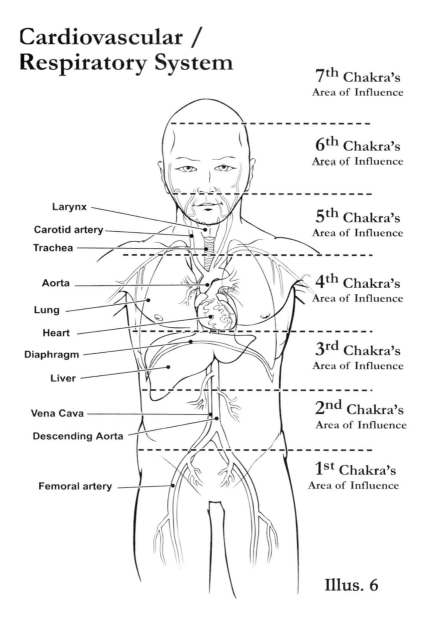

7th Chakra's
Area of Influence

6th Chakra's
Area of Influence

Larynx

Carotid artery

Trachea

5th Chakra's
Area of Influence

Aorta

Lung

Heart

4th Chakra's
Area of Influence

Diaphragm

Liver

3rd Chakra's
Area of Influence

Vena Cava

Descending Aorta

2nd Chakra's
Area of Influence

Femoral artery

1st Chakra's
Area of Influence

Illus. 6

Lymph / Immune System

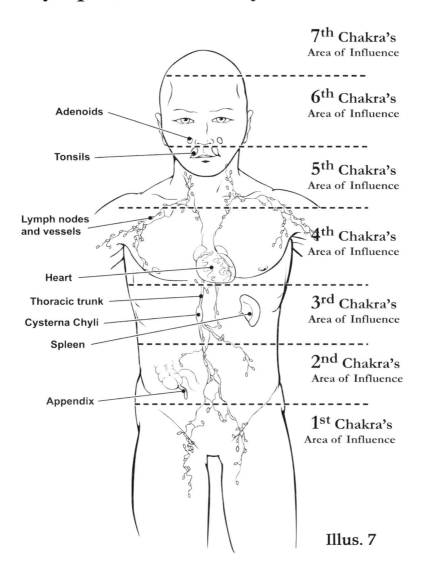

7th Chakra's Area of Influence

6th Chakra's Area of Influence

Adenoids

Tonsils

5th Chakra's Area of Influence

Lymph nodes and vessels

4th Chakra's Area of Influence

Heart

Thoracic trunk

Cysterna Chyli

Spleen

3rd Chakra's Area of Influence

2nd Chakra's Area of Influence

Appendix

1st Chakra's Area of Influence

Illus. 7

51

In a disordered mind, as in a disordered body, soundness of health is impossible.

- Cicero

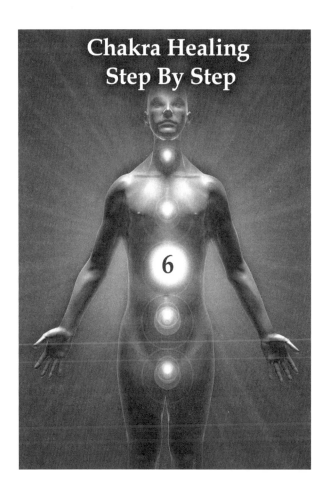

Chakra Healing Step By Step

The following are suggestions to do before receiving or performing a Chakra Healing. Follow as many on the list as you can.

- Consume only water or juice four to six hours before the Healing.

- Limit or stop use of caffeine drinks four to six hours before the Healing.
- Stop drinking alcohol 24 hours before the Healing.
- Limit sugar 24 hours before the Healing.
- Limit or stop smoking four to six hours before the Healing

Intent, Focus, Visualize

While performing a Chakra Healing, you must have strong Intent, be focused, and visualize. Intent is your state of mind in knowing what needs to be accomplished during a Chakra Healing. Focus is staying in the moment and concentrating on performing the steps during the Chakra Healing. Visualize is to form a mental image. If you have a difficult time visualizing, just know the image is there when I ask you to visualize it.

Steps Explained

Step 1.
Know which Chakra you will use during the Chakra Healing. Use the information provided in Chapter Five for this.

Step 2.
Clear the area where the Chakra Healing will be performed. This will remove any negative energy that can interfere with the Healing. I do this by smudging. Smudging is using smoke from burning herbs or plants to purify a space of negative energy. It is effective because the smoke

attaches itself to the negative energy and as the smoke clears, it takes the negative energy with it.

Most commonly used today for smudging is Sage, Cedar, and Sweet grass, which are tied in bundles called "sticks." Smudging sticks are available in New Age stores or online. To smudge, light the smudge stick in the middle of the area and then walk around waving it so the smoke spreads throughout the whole area.

If you cannot smudge, you can clear the area by visualizing golden light filling the area with the Intent to have it absorb or remove any negative energy, then have the light dissolve into the earth. If you have your own method for clearing feel free to use it. Clearing should only take few minutes.

Step 3.
Ground yourself before performing the Chakra Healing on yourself or on another person. Grounding removes any negative energy and thoughts you might have. This helps to stay focused during the Healing.

To ground yourself, stand and take several deep breaths. Then visualize golden light going very slowly through the top of your head (the 7th Chakra) all the way down through the center of your body, out both legs into the earth.

As you visualize the light moving through your body, use your Intent to have the light absorb any negative thoughts or energy you have. Once the light is in the earth, wait a few seconds and then take several deep breaths. The grounding is complete. The whole process should only take a few minutes.

Step 4.
Move to the front of the person so you can access the front of the Chakra you will be working with and start the Chakra Healing. If you are giving the Healing to yourself, the best way is to be lying down on your back when you begin. Then, when you work with a back Chakra, turn on your stomach. You can also do it sitting on a chair.

If performing the Chakra Healing on another person, the person can be lying down or sitting on a stool. If the person is sitting on a stool move into a position three to four feet in front of them so you can access the Chakra you will be working with. If the person is lying down, have them on their back and you can stand next to the Chakra you will be working with.

Step 5.
You are ready to start the Chakra Healing. The person who is receiving the Healing should close their eyes. Now state the Intent for the Chakra Healing silently if performing the Healing on yourself or another person.

The Intent is the reason why the Chakra Healing is being performed. For example, "This Chakra Healing is to help heal a kidney infection." This should only take a few seconds. You can use your own wording as long as the Intent is clear. This should only take a few seconds.

Step 6.
If performing the Chakra Healing on another person, visualize a spinning golden ball of light about the size of your fist a few inches away and over the Chakra you are working with. If giving the Chakra Healing to yourself, visualize the golden ball a few inches over your own Chakra you will be working with.

Step 7.
Lower the ball of light into the middle of the Chakra. If performing the Chakra Healing on another person or giving it to yourself, visualize this happening.

Step 8.
Visualize the spinning golden ball of light in the middle of the Chakra for about three minutes with the Intent for it to clear any blockages in the Chakra.

Step 9.
After three minutes, visualize the ball of light dissolving in the Chakra.

Step 10.
Now send Life Force into the Chakra for about two minutes. If performing the Chakra Healing on another person, direct both palms toward the Chakra you are working with. Then, visualize Universal Life Force as a white light coming from above your 7th Chakra into the Chakra, flowing through your body, out of your palms and into the Chakra to which they are directed.

If giving the Chakra Healing to yourself, you do not need to use your hands. Just visualize the Universal Life Force as a white light coming from high above the Chakra you are working with and flowing into it.

While you are sending the life force, your Intent from Step 5 will automatically direct it to the health issue that needs the Life Force for healing.

Step 11.
Next you will work with the Back Chakra. It you are performing the Healing on another person who is sitting on a stool, move behind them to access the back of the Chakra you are working with. If the person is lying down, have them turn over onto their stomach.

If giving the Chakra Healing to yourself and you are lying down, turn over and visualize the location of the back of the Chakra you are working with. Or, if you are sitting in a chair, visualize the back of the Chakra you are working with.

If working with the 7th Chakra on another person or yourself, go to Step 17 since there is no back 7th Chakra.

Step 12.
If performing the Chakra Healing on another person, visualize the same spinning golden ball of light as in Step 6 a few inches over their Back Chakra. If giving the Chakra Healing to yourself, visualize it a few inches over your Back Chakra.

Step 13.
Visualize lowering the ball of light into the middle of the Back Chakra.

Step 14.
Visualize the ball of light in the middle of the Back Chakra for about three minutes with the Intent for it to clear any blockages in the Chakra.

Step 15
After three minutes, visualize the ball of light dissolving in the Chakra.

Step 16.
Use the same directions as in Step 9. Only you will be sending Universal life force into the Back Chakra.

Step 17.
Next, if giving the Chakra Healing to yourself, take several deep breaths and then open your eyes, the Chakra Healing is complete.

If performing the Chakra Healing on another person, tell them to take several deep breaths and ask them to open their eyes. Then state the Chakra Healing is finished. Now shake or rub your hands together to break any energy connection you might still have with the person.

Every time you don't follow your inner guidance, you feel a loss of energy, loss of power, a sense of spiritual deadness.

- Shakti Gawain

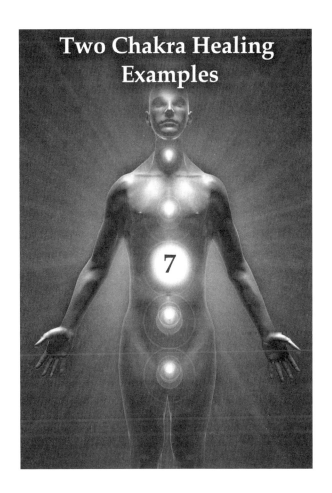

Two Chakra Healing Examples

7

Here are two Chakra Healings examples with photos and illustrations for you to study. In the first example I perform a Chakra Healing on a woman and in the second example the woman performs a Chakra Healing on herself.

Always reference Chapter Six for a detailed explanation of the steps, if needed.

In the two examples, the Chakra Healing is for a lung infection. The lungs are in the 4th Chakra's Area of Influence, so the 4th Chakra will be used during the healing.

Example One.

1. Review Illus. 6: Cardiovascular/ Respiratory System. You will find the lungs in the Area of Influence in the 4th Chakra. That will be the Chakra use in this example. (Illus. 1)

2. Clear the area. (Illus. 2)

3. Ground yourself. (Illus. 3)

4. Move to the front of the person so you can access the front side of their 4th Chakra. (Illus. 4)

5. Have the person close their eyes. State the Intent silently to yourself in your own words. For example, you could say, "This Chakra Healing is to help heal a lung infection." (Illus. 5)

6. Visualize a golden ball of spinning light a few inches in front of the Chakra you are working with. (Illus. 6)

7. Lower the spinning ball of light into the middle of the Chakra. (Illus. 7)

8. Keep the ball of light spinning in the middle of the Chakra with the Intent to clear any blockages in the Chakra for three minutes. (Illus. 8)

9. Then dissolve the ball of light in the Chakra. (Illus. 9)

10. Send Universal Life Force into the Chakra for several minutes. While you are sending the Life Force, your Intent from Step 5 will automatically direct it to the health issue that needs the Life Force for healing. (Illus. 10)

11. Move into position to access of the back of the Chakra you are working with. (Illus. 11)

12. Visualize a golden ball of spinning light in front of the Back Chakra. (Illus. 12)

13. Lower the spinning ball of light into the middle of the Back Chakra. (Illus. 13)

14. Keep the ball of light spinning in the middle of the Chakra with the Intent to clear any blockages in the Chakra for three minutes. (Illus.14)

15. Then dissolve the ball of light in the Chakra. (Illus. 15)

16. Send Universal Life Force into the Back Chakra for several minutes. While you are sending the Life Force, your Intent from Step 5 will automatically direct it to the health issue that needs the Life Force for Healing. (Illus. 16)

17. Have the person take several breaths and then open their eyes. Tell them the Chakra Healing is complete. (Illus. 17)

Cardiovascular / Respiratory System

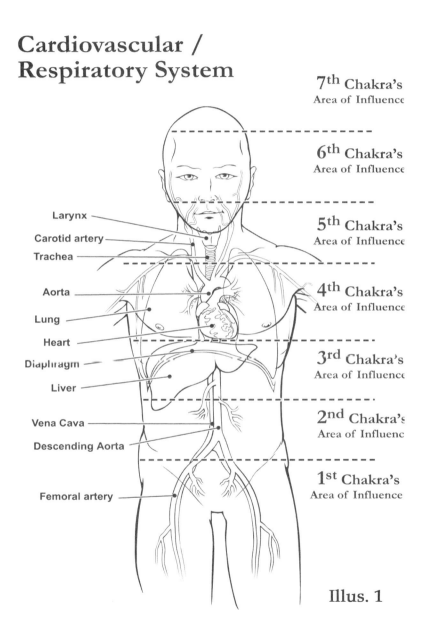

7th Chakra's
Area of Influence

6th Chakra's
Area of Influence

5th Chakra's
Area of Influence

Larynx

Carotid artery

Trachea

4th Chakra's
Area of Influence

Aorta

Lung

Heart

Diaphragm

3rd Chakra's
Area of Influence

Liver

Vena Cava

Descending Aorta

2nd Chakra's
Area of Influenc

1st Chakra's
Area of Influence

Femoral artery

Illus. 1

Illus. 2

Illus. 3

Illus. 4

Illus. 5

Illus. 6

Illus. 7

Illus. 8

Illus. 9

Illus. 10

Illus. 11

Illus. 12

Illus. 13

Illus. 14

Illus. 15

Illus. 16

Illus. 17

Example 2

1. Review Illus. 6 Cardiovascular/Respiratory System. You will find the lungs in the Area of Influence in the 4th Chakra. That will be the Chakra use in this example. (Illus. 18)

2. Clear the area. (Illus. 19)

3. Ground yourself. (Illus. 20)

4. Be in a position so you can visualize the front side of the 4th Chakra on the front of your body. If you are lying down, you must lie on your back. You can also do this while sitting on a stool. (Illus. 21)

5. Close your eyes and state the Intent in your own words silently to yourself for the Chakra Healing. For example, "This Chakra Healing is to help heal my lung infection." (Illus. 22)

6. Visualize a golden ball of spinning light in a few inches in front of the Chakra you are working with. (Illus. 23)

7. Lower the spinning ball of light into the middle of the Chakra. (Illus. 24)

8. Keep the ball of light spinning in the middle of the Chakra for three minutes with the Intent to clear any blockages in the Chakra. (Illus. 25)

9. After three minutes, dissolve the ball of light in the Chakra. (Illus. 26)

10. Send Universal Life Force into the Chakra for several minutes. While you are sending the Life Force, your Intent from Step 5 will automatically direct it to the health issue that needs the Life Force for Healing. (Illus. 27)

11. Turn over and visualize the location of the back of the Chakra you are working with. (Illus. 28)

12. Visualize a golden ball of spinning light in front of the Back Chakra. (Illus. 29)

13. Lower the spinning ball of light into the middle of the Back Chakra. (Illus. 30)

14. Keep the ball of light spinning in the middle of the Chakra for three minutes with the intent to clear any blockages in the Chakra. (Illus. 31)

15. After three minutes, dissolve the ball of light in the Chakra. (Illus. 32)

16. Send Universal Life Force into the Back Chakra for several minutes. While you are sending the Life Force, your Intent from Step 5 will automatically direct it to the health issue that needs the Life Force for Healing. (Illus. 33)

17. Take several breaths and open your eyes. The Chakra Healing is complete. (Illus. 34)

Cardiovascular / Respiratory System

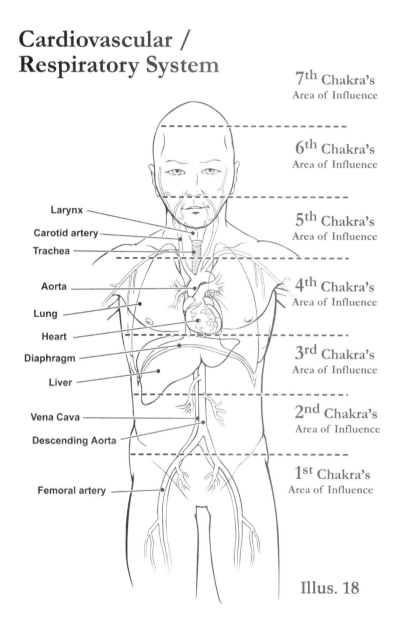

7th Chakra's
Area of Influence

6th Chakra's
Area of Influence

5th Chakra's
Area of Influence

Larynx

Carotid artery

Trachea

4th Chakra's
Area of Influence

Aorta

Lung

Heart

Diaphragm

3rd Chakra's
Area of Influence

Liver

Vena Cava

2nd Chakra's
Area of Influence

Descending Aorta

1st Chakra's
Area of Influence

Femoral artery

Illus. 18

Illus. 19

Illus. 20

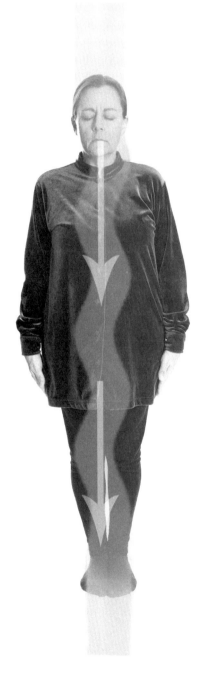

Illus. 21

Illus. 22

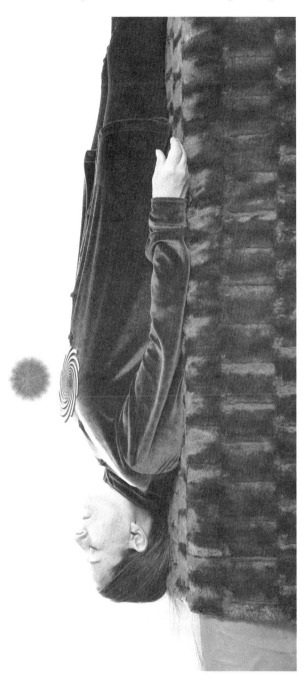

Illus. 23

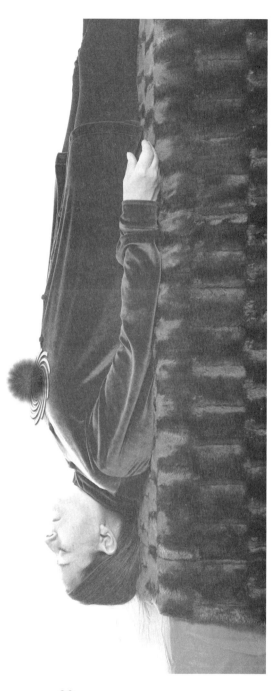

Illus. 24

Illus. 25

Illus. 26

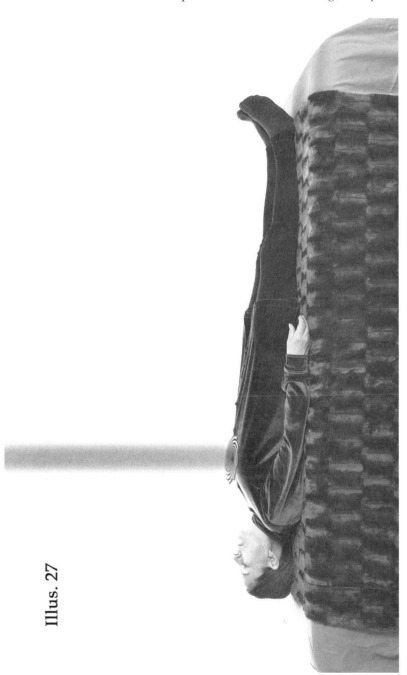

Illus. 27

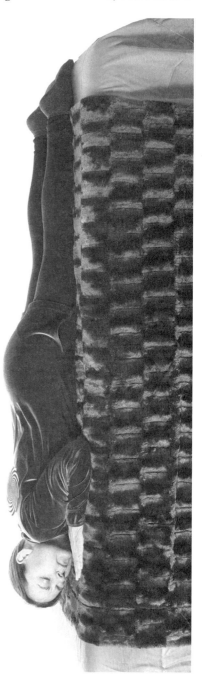

Illus. 28

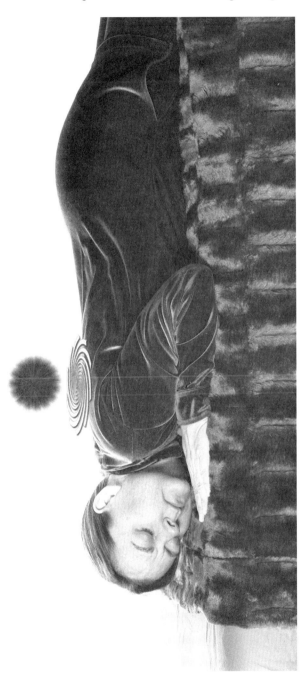

Illus. 29

Illus. 30

Illus. 31

Illus. 32

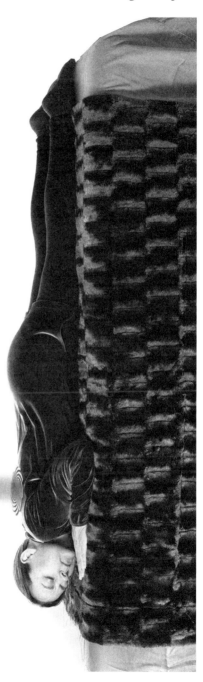

Illus. 33

Illus. 34

There is deep wisdom within our very flesh, if we can only come to our senses and feel it.

- Elizabeth A. Behnke

Life is not merely to be alive, but to be well.

- Marcus Valerius Martial

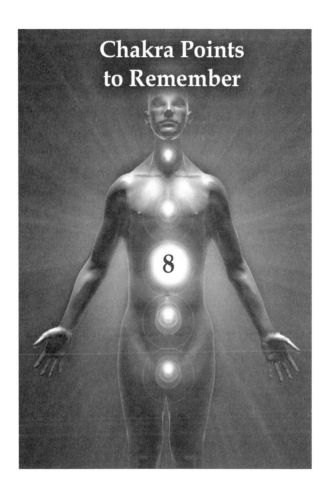

The following are points you should remember about Chakra Healing. Read each point several times and always refer back to points list if you have any questions.

- You should have a quiet environment when performing a Chakra Healing session.

- Maintain strong intent and focus throughout the Chakra Healing session.

- During a session, talk only when necessary so you will not be distracted.

- If you feel the need to channel the Life Energy longer than five minutes, by all means do so. Just stop sending the energy when you intuitively feel it is time to stop.

- When sending Life Energy during a Chakra Healing, you can use one or two palms.

- While sending the Life Energy you might feel sensations of heat, cold, or vibrations in your palms. If this happens, do not worry. It is part of the process. Or, you might not experience any sensations while sending the Life Energy. Either way, the Life Energy is being sent.

- Review the Chakra Healing steps a few times before you actually perform your first Chakra Healing session.

- A nerve plexus is a network of intersecting nerves that come together to supply a particular area with nerves.

- An organ is a structure that contains at least two different types of tissue functioning together for a common purpose.

- Once you become experienced performing a Chakra Healing, it should never last longer than fifteen to thirty minutes.

- Chakra Healing is only for physical ailments or and/or diseases. For mental or emotional issues, perform an Aura Healing.

- What makes one Chakra Healing different from another Chakra Healing even though the same Chakra is used? It's the Intent used for the specific ailment or disease during the Healing.

- Perform a Chakra Healing only if you know the physical ailment and/or disease it is for and where it has manifested in the physical body. With this information you can determine which Chakra to use during the Healing.

- Since every person has different health circumstances, the number of Chakra Healings needed for a health issue will vary with each person.

- Perform only one Chakra Healing for one ailment or disease at a time. Then wait a minimum of three days before performing another Chakra Healing.

- You can receive as many Chakra Healings as needed for a specific ailment or disease every three days.

- Because of individual health circumstances, everyone progresses differently with regard to the time it takes to heal.

- There might come a time an ailment or disease falls into a gray area in deciding which Chakra to use during a Healing. If this happens, just take a few minutes and use your intuitiveness to decide which Chakra to use.

- After a Chakra Healing, the body will be detoxifying, so drink plenty of water during that time to help your body flush out the toxins that are released.

- After receiving a Chakra Healing take it easy for at least a few hours after the session. This allows the Life Energy to filter throughout the Chakra's Area of Influence that was worked on during the session.

- A person can also experience increased body waste elimination for a brief period after the Chakra Healing session.

- For minor health problems, one or two Chakra Healing sessions should suffice. Serious or chronic health challenges will need additional sessions.

Aura Segment

The aura given out by a person or object is as much a part of them as their flesh...

- Lucian Freud

Aura Defined

Before we begin with my teachings of the Aura, I need to mention that there is other literature that exists with regard to interpretations and descriptions of the Aura and some may differ from mine.

If you find that in the previous Aura information you have studied and/or read is diverse from mine, do not worry about it. All Aura teachings do agree on one point -- there is a Mental and Emotional Layer that exists inside the Aura and that is the main focus and key element in my Aura Healing method.

Aura History

For thousands of years to today, many cultures around the word have known of an energy field that exists around our physical bodies. Ancient Hindus, Buddhists, Greeks, and Romans depicted this energy field in paintings of significant people and Gods. You also have the halo that is reflected in the art of Christians throughout history to the present day which some people believe represents this energy field. The energy field surrounding the physical body is now commonly called the "Aura." From Buddhist priests to Native American shamans, many spiritual leaders of various doctrines throughout history and to this day have incorporated the Aura into their religious and healing modalities.

Aura is a Latin word meaning "light" or "glow of light." One dictionary defines the Aura as "invisible vapor that seems to arise from and surround a person or thing." The most common scientific belief is the Aura is a subtle energy field surrounding the human body created by molecules and atoms. As these elements interact they create a subtle multi-dimensional energy field. All living things, including flowers and trees, have an Aura, although not as complex as the Human Aura.

The majority of people cannot see the Aura, although experienced Healers can sense and feel its presence. Although there is a select group of people who can naturally see the Aura, the abilities of this group range from seeing just a hazy mist around the body to seeing the actual Aura. People who can see the entire Aura describe it as an egg or bubble shape of hazy, shimmering light in a rainbow of colors around the physical body.

My Aura Healing method does not require one to see the Aura and its colors, but most students always like to try to see the Aura if possible. With that in mind, I will explain a process to see another person's Aura, as well as your own, in a later chapter. In the next chapter I will explain the Human Aura.

Emotion always has its roots in the unconscious and manifests itself in the body.
- Irene Claremont de Castillejo

I believe the Human Aura is a composite of seven layers surrounding the physical body. Some teachings describe more layers, but most will include a variation of these seven layers.

These layers are also called "auric layers, subtle bodies, energy fields, energy bodies, or bodies." Throughout this book I will use the term "layer."

Each layer relates to the physical, mental, emotional, and spiritual aspects of the person. Each layer consists of vibrating energy frequencies which can change, depending on the state of the layer. These states will depend on the physical, mental, emotional, and spiritual conditions of the person and the circumstances they are experiencing at any given moment. All seven layers occupy the same space surrounding each other in successive layers, with each layer extending out beyond the last. The layers are interconnected and reliant on the other layers for their normal function. At the same time, all layers function interactively with the physical body.

The first three layers interface with material or physical needs of the body and also relate to the mind, ideas, emotions, health, and desires. The fourth layer acts as a buffer and intermediary between the others. These four layers are the ones you will interact with when performing an Aura Healing. The outer three layers interface and relate with your spiritual needs, your soul, and spirit.
Most Human Auras extend from the body about five feet, although with more spiritually evolved and developed individuals, Auras can extend outward perhaps seven feet or more.

You are not just a physical body with an Aura surrounding you. You are an Aura with a physical body and both together comprise one complete being. So let's talk about the physical body first before I describe the Seven Layers of the Aura.

Physical Body

The Aura's seven energy layers surrounding the physical body. The physical body (Illus. 35) is the most tangible part of our being and provides the stability and solid foundation for the Aura. The physical body helps us in the moment to be conscious of our environment and to walk, talk, eat, etc. It is our transportation for our journey through life. As I mentioned before and it is an important point to remember, the physical body surrounded by an Aura equals one complete being. The physical body also has the brain, which functions, in part, as a medium or relay switch to translate and process emotional and mental information coming and going throughout your complete being.

The physical body is an ongoing barometer on how healthy and balanced you are during your journey in this life, although this physical barometer sometimes does not reflect in real time your state of health. For example, if you cut your finger, you know your state of health immediately, but if you have emotional or mental issues that are not being addressed, symptoms will eventually manifest in your physical body in the future. The good news is that with the information (symptoms) you receive from your physical body, you can make the necessary changes and/ or Healing needed to stay in a healthy, balanced state in both your Aura and physical body.

Etheric Layer

The first layer is the Etheric Layer (Illus. 36). "Etheric" is derived from the word "ether" and in Metaphysics, ether refers to a state between energy and matter. This layer extends up to two inches away from the body. Being the first layer closest to the body, it fits like a second skin and is in constant motion. This layer is the map or blueprint for the physical body. It holds impressions of all the organs, glands, Chakras, and Meridians. It is where the Life Force can be felt or sensed as it flows through Meridians and Chakras. Physical signs of illness and injury can also be detected in this layer by scanning. "Scanning is a process Healers use when they pass their hands a few inches above the body. People who can see this layer say it usually appears as shades of blue or gray when it is healthy.

Emotional Layer

The second layer is the Emotional Layer (Ilus. 37) and it extends about two to four inches away from the physical body. The Emotional Layer is a swirling mass of energy that reflects the feelings and emotions we have and experience. It is always in a state of flux because our emotions and feelings are constantly changing due to our circumstances in life and how we perceive them. The layer loosely resembles the human shape, but is not as defined as the Etheric Layer. All emotions -- happiness, hope, love, anger, sorrow, hate -- are in this layer. It also stores all unresolved emotions, including fear, resentment, anger, loneliness, and so forth. The state of the Emotional Layer affects the Etheric Layer, which in turn affects the physical body. The Emotional Layer expresses the state of the Mental Layer, which is the next layer out. People who can see this layer describe it as a purple or violet color when healthy.

Mental Layer

The third layer is the Mental Layer (Illus. 38) and extends about four to eight inches away from the physical body. This layer contains our thoughts, ideas, beliefs, logic, and intellect. It also contains our mental processes and reflects the conscious mind at any moment. In this layer, thought, intellect, and ideas are formulated and authenticated. Mental health and/or unresolved mental issues are also reflected here. The Mental Layer's information resonates down to the emotional body, which reacts to it with your programmed emotional responses. However, these programmed emotional responses to situations and circumstances can be changed and sometimes must be changed for a healthy physical state to be possible. Aura Healing can help with this. People who can see this layer describe the color as a bright shade of yellow that becomes brighter when a person is focusing on a mental process.

Astral Layer

The Astral Layer is the fourth layer (Illus. 39) and it extends about eight to twelve inches away from the physical body. This layer separates the first three layers from the outer three layers. The Astral Layer is the bridge or portal between the physical world and the spiritual plane. The connection to the physical world is your body and the first three Aura Layers. The Astral layer is important in performing Aura Healing and you will be working within this layer. People who can see the Astral Layer state it is a brightly colored rosy hue.

The connection to the spiritual plane is the next three layers beyond the Astral Layer.

The distances of the first four layers are about the same for all people up to about a foot. The next three layers extend out from the first four layers anywhere from one to five feet, the distances depending on a person's spiritual development. These three layers distances will expand as a person's spiritual awareness increases.

Etheric Template Layer

The fifth layer is the Etheric Template Layer (Illus. 40) and it extends about one to two feet away from the physical body. Its primary function is to keep the Etheric Layer (first layer) in place and it contains a template of the physical body on a higher spiritual level. This layer also contains your unique inner identity, the essence of your present state of being. The most common perception of this color is a dark blue or cobalt blue.

Celestial Layer

The sixth layer is the Celestial Layer (Illus. 41). It extends about two to three feet away from the body. It is the layer where we can experience unconditional love and spiritual ecstasy. It's the layer of feelings and emotions within the world of our spirit. Basically, it is the layer of spiritual emotions in the spiritual plane. Group consciousness and universal love are also experienced in this layer. People who can see this layer describe its color as green when it is healthy.

Ketheric Layer

The seventh layer is the Ketheric Layer (Illus. 42) and it extends about three to five feet away from the body, depending on your spiritual state, although it can expand as your spirituality awareness increases. The energies in this layer vibrate at the highest frequency of all the layers. People who can see or sense this layer say it forms an oval similar to an egg which surrounds and protects the other Aura Layers within it. With developed spiritual awareness, this form changes to more of a circle. It is believed that this layer can become a perfect circle when a person achieves their highest spiritual awareness. Such a level of awareness is achieved by only a very few individuals. This is the ultimate layer that is immortal, all knowing, and through this layer we can become one with our source. It is our spiritual template. Through this layer the soul communicates with the conscious mind via the subconscious mind in the mental body. While the other layers will dissipate in time, this layer will always exist, even after death. After death, it is believed this layer can reincarnate in the Aura of a newly formed physical body. With the information accumulated in the previous life available for guidance in the new life. People who can see this layer describe it as an extremely bright golden light that is rapidly pulsating. This golden light is composed of tiny gold and silver threads spreading throughout the layer.

Auras Interact

As I mentioned before, it is a challenge for most people to see Auras, but the majority of people have felt or sensed their presence in themselves and others at one time or another. Through Auras we feel and sense feelings, emotions, thoughts, memories, and other non-physical experiences, even though you may not have connected this to your Aura when this was occurring.

The Aura is very sensitive and we pick up these feelings and emotions when we come within range of another person's Aura. How many times have you met a person and instantly felt uncomfortable around them? Or the opposite — you met a person and felt immediately at ease in their presence? Maybe you came in contact with a person and instantly knew what state they were in emotionally — sad, happy, in love, or their attitude — good or bad. There are many expressions to describe this: "...the person gives me the creeps," "I feel good or bad vibes," "I feel funny about the person," "…the person's energy is good/bad," "…the person doesn't feel right," and so on. This information is coming from your Auras interacting, especially the Mental and Emotional Layers.

Auras can also attract situations and circumstances. A negative example would be if a person has a fear issue within the emotional layer, they will often be drawn to circumstances which reaffirm this fear. A positive example of this is if a person has a strong love regarding something, they can be drawn to circumstances and situations which reaffirm this love.

The next chapter I will talk about the purpose and goal of Aura Healing.

Illus. 35   Physical Body

Illus. 36   Etheric Layer

Illus. 37   Emotional Layer

Illus. 38   Mental Layer

Illus. 39   **Astral Layer**

Illus. 40   Etheric Template Layer

Illus. 41   Celestial Layer

Illus. 42   Ketheric Layer

Some patients I see are actually draining into their bodies the diseased thoughts of their minds.
- Zacharty Bercovitz

Purpose of an
Aura Healing

11

Unresolved emotional and mental issues that are reflected in the Emotional and Mental Layers of the Aura can form blockages. These blockages are what I call "Psychic Debris." Psychic Debris is also called different names by Healers, such as "emotional or mental blocks" and "negative thought forms." Whatever it's called, all Healers agree that Psychic Debris exists.

Normally, if resolved or released in a timely manner, emotional and mental issues will not become Psychic Debris. However, if they are not resolved or released, they become Psychic Debris. This is when problems start to manifest. The emotional or mental issue that created the Psychic Debris can become chronic and negatively affect your life. If the Psychic Debris is not removed, it can resonate down from the Aura to the physical body and cause illness and disease.

Aura Healing removes Psychic Debris so the emotional or mental issue that created the debris can be resolved or released and will not resonate down to the physical body and manifest as a physical ailment or disease. Once an ailment and/or disease has manifested in the physical body, you can perform a Chakra Healing, which is explained in the first segment of the book.

If possible, it is best to perform Aura Healing and remove Psychic Debris from the Aura before it affects the physical body. People who can see Psychic Debris describe it as darkness spread throughout the first four layers of the Aura with most of the darkness in the Emotional and Mental Layers.

Aura Healing Experiences

Students and clients always like to know what they should experience during an Aura Healing session. It is human nature to want to be conscious of signs to confirm something is actually happening during an Aura Healing. The majority of the time there are indeed obvious signs and indications during an Aura Healing experienced by the person receiving it and/ or giving it, but, occasionally there are either minimal signs or no signs experienced during the Healing session. Please do not worry or be concerned about this when and if this happens. It does not mean the Aura Healing will not be successful. When there are minimal signs, or none of which you are consciously aware during the Aura Healing, the same results will manifest as with there are perceptible physical experiences. I will describe signs that can manifest during an Aura Healing.

Signs During the Healing

During an Aura Healing the signs (experiences) are unique and different each time for the person receiving it and even with the Healer performing it. The reason for this is simple: A person's Aura, especially the Mental and Emotional Layers, is constantly changing and evolving either in a positive or negative direction. Plus, every person's circumstances are different regarding why the Aura Healing is needed. All of these variables make each and every Aura Healing session unique. To avoid the possibility of fear or surprise, I recommend mentioning to the person who is to receive an Aura Healing that they could possibly experience some of these "signs" during an Aura Healing:

- Tingling sensations, warmth or cold around the body
- Heat from the direction where the Aura Healing is being performed
- Flashes and/ or pulsating around the physical body in the Aura
- Mental thoughts and memories rushing up to the conscious mind about the issues for which the Healing is being performed
- Physical body feeling lighter
- Feelings of unconditional love
- Flashes of insight and knowing about the issue for which the Aura Healing is being performed.
- Relaxed feeling or tingly, vibrating sensations in the Aura or the physical body
- Spiritual visions
- Out-of-body experiences
- Colors visualized or sensed, music heard, and/or different aromas smelled
- Crying, nose running, and various fluids released from the physical body

The signs experienced may be only one or a combination of the above, or the person may experience their own unique signs. Maybe nothing will be consciously experienced at all during the Aura Healing. If this happens, it does not mean the Aura Healing has not been received or it will not work. There will be the same results either way if the Aura Healing is performed correctly.

After receiving an Aura Healing, the body may feel lighter and one might feel like time is moving differently for a while. The whole Aura Healing may even seem like a dream. Everyone progresses in an individual manner in terms of healing because of their individual circumstances. In fact, as I mentioned above, after an Aura Healing you might not consciously sense or physically feel anything at first, but change will be taking place in your Aura.

Eventually you will start to sense and feel the change in the issue for which you received the Aura Healing. It might be subtle at first, but as time goes on, you will have more conscious awareness of a change and you may need to receive additional Aura Healings for other issues.

The more you consistently choose loving, appreciative thoughts, the more your aura radiates out that energy of love and appreciation.

- Karen Whitaker

**Aura Healing
Step by Step**

12

Here are some suggestions I recommend doing before receiving or performing Aura Healing. Follow as many on the list as you can.

- Consume only water or juice four to six hours before the Healing

- Limit or stop use of caffeine drinks four to six hours before the Healing
- Stop drinking alcohol 24 hours before the Healing
- Limit sugar 24 hours before the Healing
- Limit or stop smoking four to six hours before the Healing

Intent, Focus, Visualize

While performing the Aura Healing, you must have strong Intent, be focused, and visualize. Intent is the state of mind in knowing what the exact purpose of the Healing Aura is for and what needs to be accomplished during the Aura Healing. Focus is staying in the moment and concentrating on performing the steps during the Aura Healing. Visualize is to form a mental image. If you have a difficult time visualizing, just know the image is there when I ask you to visualize it.

Four Layers

During the Aura Healing, you will only be working within the first four layers of the Aura. That's where the Emotional and Mental Layers are and where Psychic Debris manifests.

Psychic Debris in the Emotional Layer always overlaps into the Mental Layer. Psychic Debris in the Mental Layer always overlaps into the Emotional Layer. Psychic Debris can also be in the Etheric Layer if it is starting to resonate down into the physical body. It can even spread out into the Astral Layer.

Steps Explained

Step 1.

Intent is the key factor in a successful Aura Healing, so before performing Aura Healing on another person or giving it to yourself, you must know the Intent for the healing. The Intent is determined by the emotional or mental issue that is causing problems in a person's life. If the issue is causing problems and the person is aware of it, most likely it has manifested into Psychic Debris, so you need to ask the person what the Aura Healing is for and they will tell you. With some people it might take a little coaxing on your part, but eventually they will tell you. Most people are anxious to share what they need to be healed so acquiring this information from them should not be a problem.

If the Aura Healing is for yourself, then you know what the Intent for the Aura Healing should be.

Use the following examples as guidelines to help formulate Intent for Aura Healings. You do not need to know if the root cause of an issue for the Aura Healing is emotional or mental. The Aura Healing will remove all Psychic Debris stated in the Intent no matter if it originated in the Emotional Layer or the Mental Layer. Of course you are going to come across many issues, but use the following examples as guidelines.

Issue: Fear of a Father
The Intent would be to remove the Psychic Debris created by the fear of one's father.

Issue: Anger towards a relative
The Intent would be to remove the Psychic Debris created by anger towards one's relative.

Issue: Fear of flying
The Intent would be to remove the Psychic Debris created by the stress caused by fear of flying.

Issue: Cannot lose weight
The Intent would be to remove the Psychic Debris that keeps a person from losing weight.

Issue: Cannot Stop Smoking
The Intent would be to remove the Psychic Debris that keeps a person from being able to stop smoking.

Issue: Cannot stop eating sugar
The Intent would be to remove the Psychic Debris that keeps a person from being able to stop eating sugar.

Issue: Anxiety from shyness
The Intent would be to remove the Psychic Debris created by the anxiety of being shy.

Issue: Depression from moving
The Intent would be to remove the Psychic Debris created by depression caused by moving.

Issue: Guilt regarding divorce
The Intent would be to remove the Psychic Debris created by the guilt of getting divorced.

Issue: Unrequited love from a boyfriend/girlfriend
The intent would be to remove the Psychic Debris created by unrequited love from a boyfriend or girlfriend.

Issue: Panic regarding speaking in public
The Intent would be to remove the Psychic Debris created by panic when speaking in public.

Issue: Fear of water
The Intent would be to remove the Psychic Debris created by the fear of water.

Issue: Jealousy regarding a co-worker
The Intent would be to remove the Psychic Debris created by feeling jealous about a co-worker.

Issue: Disappointment over losing a job
The Intent would be to remove the Psychic Debris caused by the disappointment over losing a job.

Step 2.
Clear the area where the Aura Healing is to be performed. This will remove any negative energy that can interfere with the Healing. I do this by smudging.

Smudging is using smoke from burning herbs or plants to purify a space of negative energy.

It is effective because the smoke attaches itself to the negative energy and as the smoke clears, it takes negative energy with it.

Most commonly used today for smudging is Sage, Cedar, and Sweet grass which are tied in bundles called "sticks." Smudging sticks are available in New Age stores or online. To smudge, light the smudge stick in the middle of the area and then walk around waving the stick so the smoke spreads throughout the whole area.

If you cannot smudge, you can clear the area by visualizing golden light filling the area with the Intent to have it absorb or remove any negative energy, then have the light dissolve into the earth. If you have your own method for clearing, feel free to use it. Clearing should only take few minutes.

Step 3.
Ground yourself before performing the Aura Healing on yourself or another person. Grounding removes any negative energy and thoughts you might have. This helps to stay focused during the Healing.

To ground yourself, stand and take several deep breaths. Then visualize golden light going very slowly through the top of your head, (the 7th Chakra), all the way down through the center of your body and out both legs into the earth.

As you visualize the light moving through your body, use your Intent to have the light absorb any negative thoughts or energy you have. Once the light is in the earth, wait a few seconds and then take several deep breaths. The grounding is complete. The whole process should only take a few minutes.

Step 4.

Move into position to perform the Aura Healing. The position must provide you with access to the front side of the person's body. If you are giving the Aura Healing to yourself, the best way is to be lying down on your back when you begin. Then, when you work with the back of the Aura, you should turn over onto your stomach. You can also give yourself the Aura Healing sitting on a chair.

If performing the Aura Healing on another person, the person can be lying down or sitting on a stool. If the person is sitting on a stool, move about three to four feet directly in front of them. If the person is lying down on their back, stand next to and above them.

Step 5.

You are ready to start the Aura Healing. The person who is receiving the Healing should close their eyes now. Next state the Intent for the Aura Healing silently to yourself before you start the Healing. This should only take a few seconds. I give examples on how to help formulate Intent in Step One. You can use your own wording as long as the Intent is clear, but let me suggest that you always personalize the Intent by using a name or "me," "my" or "I."

Here are two examples of personalized Intent when performing Aura Healing on another person.

- "I am going to remove the Psychic Debris from John's Aura that keeps him from losing weight."

- "I am going to remove the Psychic Debris from Sue's Aura created by her anger towards her brother Jim."

Here are two examples of personalized Intent Aura Healing on yourself.

- "I will remove the Psychic Debris from my Aura that keeps me from losing weight."

- "I will remove the Psychic Debris in my Aura created by my anger towards my brother Jim."

Step 6.
If performing the Aura Healing on another person, visualize a spinning black hole about the size of a dinner plate and about 14-16 inches out in front of the person's upper chest. This distance inches ensures that you are outside the Astral layer.

If giving the healing to yourself, just visualize the spinning black hole the same distance out in front of your upper chest. The black hole I want you to visualize will be similar in concept to a black hole in space that pulls in all space debris near it, only the spinning hole you visualize will pull in Psychic Debris. Visualize the black hole spinning for about three minutes.

While the black hole is spinning, your Intent from Step Five will automatically ensure the Psychic Debris stated in the Intent will be pulled into the black hole from the first four layers of the Aura. Most of the Psychic Debris will come from the Emotional and Mental Layers.

Step 7
Visualize the black hole with the Psychic Debris dissolving and in its place visualize a spinning ball of golden light. Keep the ball of light spinning with the Intent for the golden light to heal the Aura where the Psychic Debris was removed.

Step 8
After about two minutes, visualize the ball of light dissolving in the Aura.

Step 9
Now you want to remove Psychic Debris in the back of the Aura. If you are performing the Aura Healing on another person and they are sitting on a stool, move into a position in back of them. If the person is lying down, have them turn over and stay where you are. If you are performing the Aura Healing on yourself and you are lying down, turn over and visualize your back. If you are sitting in a chair, visualize your back.

Step 10.
This is the same as in Step 6, except you are using the back side of the Aura and, of course, you will be in a position to access their backside to do so. Visualize the spinning black hole about 14-16 inches from the back side, upper part of the person's body on whom you are performing the Aura Healing. Or, if you are performing the Aura Healing on yourself, visualize the spinning black hole out the same distance from your upper back.

Step 11

Visualize the black hole with the Psychic Debris dissolving and in its place visualize a spinning ball of golden light. Keep the ball of light spinning with the Intent for the golden light to heal the Aura where the Psychic Debris was removed.

Step 12

After about two minutes, visualize the ball of light dissolving in the Aura.

Step 13.

If performing the Aura Healing on yourself, take several deep breaths and then open your eyes. The Aura Healing is complete. If performing the Aura Healing on another person, tell them to take several deep breaths and then open their eyes. Then state "the Aura Healing is finished."

Never apologize for showing feeling. When you do so, you apologize for the truth.

- Benjamin Disraeli

Let's not forget that the little emotions are the great captains of our lives and we obey them without realizing it.

- Vincent Van Gogh

Two Aura Healing
Examples

13

Here are two Aura Healings examples with photos and illustrations for you to study. In the first example, I perform an Aura Healing on a woman and in the second example the woman performs an Aura Healing on herself.

In the two examples, the Issue for the Aura Healing is to remove the Psychic Debris created by anger towards the person's mother. Always reference Chapter 12 for a detailed explanation of the steps if needed.

Example 1

1. Know the Issue why the Aura Healing is being performed. In this example, it is to remove the Psychic Debris created by anger towards the person's mother.

2. Clear the Area. (Illus. 43)

3. Ground yourself. (Illus. 44)

4. Move into position so you will have access to the front side of the person's body. (Illus. 45)

5. Have the person close their eyes. State the Intent for the Aura Healing silently to yourself in your own words. For example, "This Aura Healing session is to remove any and all Psychic Debris in this person's Aura created by their anger towards their mother." (Illus. 46)

6. Visualize a spinning black hole about 14-16 inches away from the person's upper chest for about three minutes. The Intent from Step 5 will automatically pull the Psychic Debris into the black hole. (Illus. 47)

7. After the three minutes, visualize the spinning black hole turning into a spinning golden ball with the Intent to heal where the Psychic Debris was removed. Do this for two minutes. (Illus. 48)

8. After the two minutes, dissolve the golden ball in the Aura. (Illus. 49)

9. Next you will work with the back part of the Aura. If the person is sitting on a stool, move behind them to access the back of the Aura (Illus. 50). If the person is lying down, have them turn over onto their stomach so you will be above them.

10. Visualize a spinning black hole about 14-16 inches away from the person's upper chest on their back side for about three minutes. The Intent from Step 5 will automatically pull the Psychic Debris into the black hole. (Illus. 51)

11. Next, for two minutes, visualize the black hole turning into a spinning golden ball with the Intent to heal where the Psychic Debris was removed. (Illus. 52)

12. After two minutes, dissolve the golden ball. (Illus. 53)

13. Have the person take two breaths and then open their eyes. State "the Aura Healing is complete." (Illus. 54)

Illus. 43

Illus. 44

Illus. 45

Illus. 46

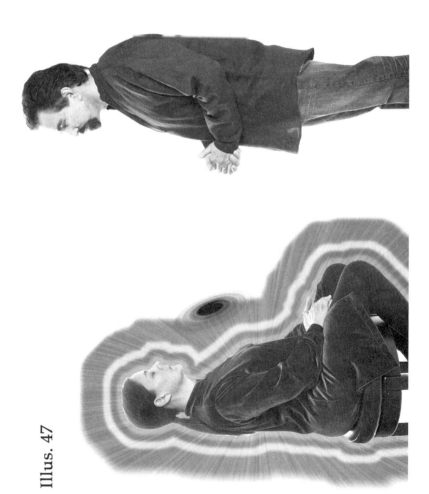

Illus. 47

Illus. 48

Illus. 49

Illus. 50

Illus. 51

Illus. 52

Illus. 53

Illus. 54

Example 2

1. Know the Issue why you are performing the Aura Healing on yourself. In this example, it is to remove the Psychic Debris created by anger you have towards your mother.

2. Clear the Area. (Illus. 55)

3. Ground yourself. (Illus. 56)

4. Be in a position so you can visualize the Aura of the front of your body. If you are lying down, you must lie on your back. (Illus. 57) You can also do this while sitting on a stool.

5. Close your eyes. State the Intent for the Aura Healing silently to yourself in your own words. For example, "This Aura Healing session is to remove any and all Psychic Debris in my Aura created by the anger I have towards my mother." (Illus. 58)

6. Visualize a spinning black hole about 14-16 inches away from your upper chest for about three minutes. The Intent from Step 5 will automatically pull the Psychic Debris into the spinning black hole. (Illus. 59)

7. After the three minutes, visualize the spinning black hole turning into a spinning golden ball with the Intent to heal where the Psychic Debris was removed. Do this for two minutes. (Illus. 60)

8. After two minutes, dissolve the golden ball in the Aura. (Illus. 61)

9. Next, you will work with the back part of your Aura. (Illus. 62) If you are lying down, turn over onto your stomach. If you are sitting on a stool, just visualize your back.

10. Visualize a spinning black hole about 14-16 inches away from your upper chest on your back side for about three minutes. (Illus. 63) The intent from Step 5 will automatically pull the Psychic Debris into the black hole.

11. Next, for two minutes, visualize the black hole turning into a spinning golden ball with the Intent to heal where the Psychic Debris was removed. (Illus. 64)

12. After two minutes, dissolve the golden ball. (Illus. 65)

13. Take two breaths and then open your eyes. The Aura healing is complete. (Illus. 66)

Illus. 55

Illus. 56

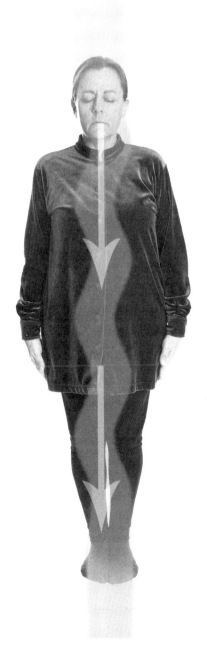

Illus. 57

Illus. 58

169

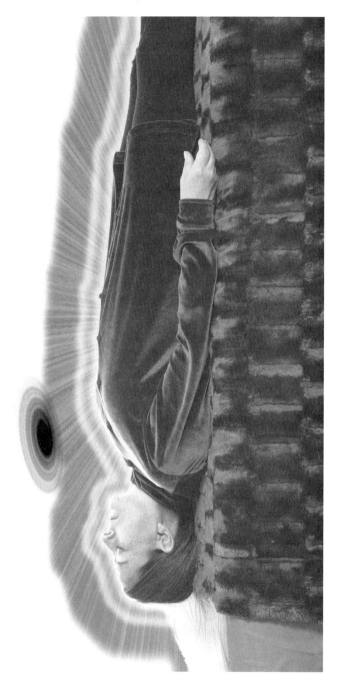

Illus. 59

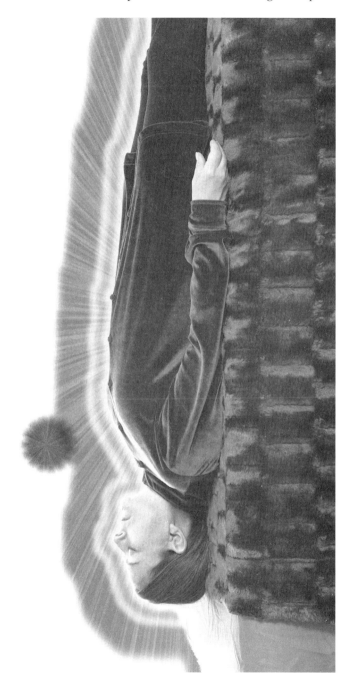

Illus. 60

171

Illus. 61

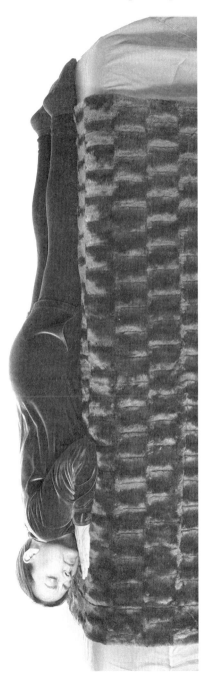

Illus. 62

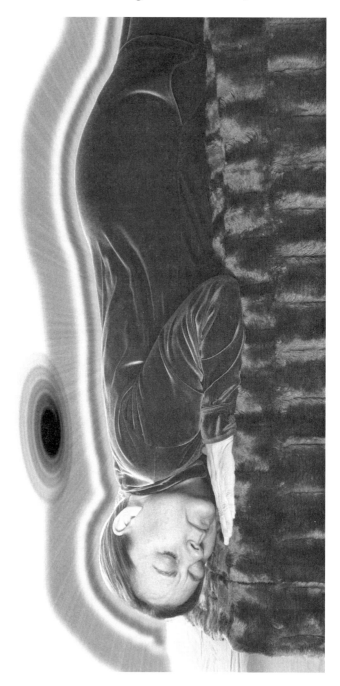

Illus. 63

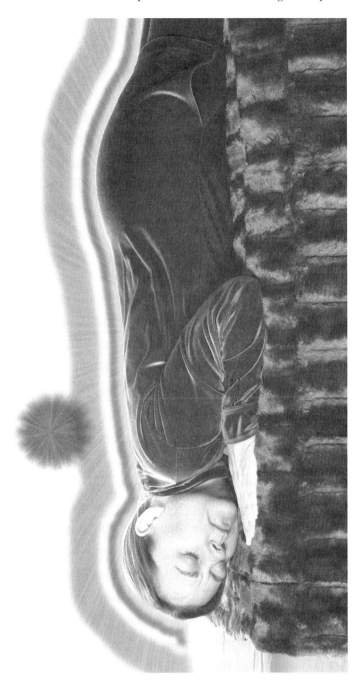

Illus. 64

175

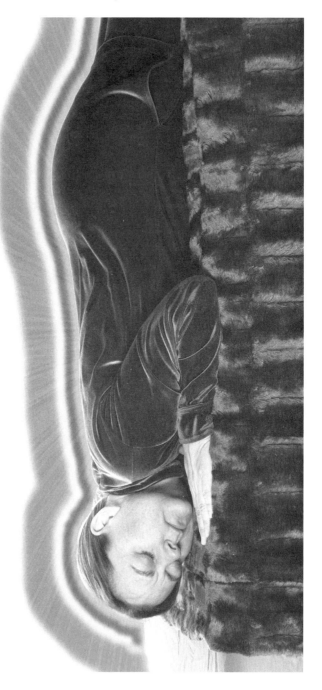

Illus. 65

Illus. 66

Beyond my body my veins are invisible.

- Antonio Porchia

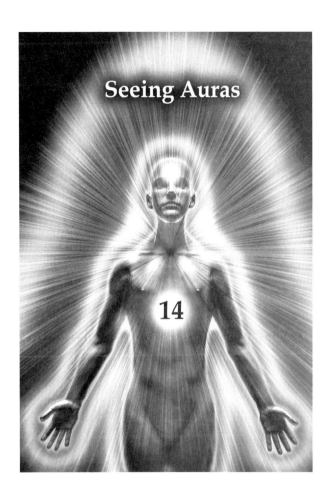

Seeing Auras

14

Students always like to try to see Auras. With that in mind, I will explain two techniques to see the Aura. There are many techniques for seeing the Aura. I believe the two I explain are the best.

The first technique is to see the Aura around others. The second one is to see the Aura around yourself. When using either one of these techniques, the majority of people will only be able to see a glow, a haze, or a mist around the body. You might fall into the select group of people who can also see Aura colors. Before I explain the techniques, here are a few guidelines to remember in seeing the Aura:

- Do not confuse the Aura with the lights seen by people suffering from migraine headaches, bright spots when the eyes are rubbed or the particles (floaters) that sometimes drift into your field of vision.
- Most people cannot see the Aura at all until they practice a method to do so. With practice, the majority will only be able to see a glow, a haze, or a mist around the body; but you might fall into the select group who can see or sense Aura colors.
- Even after practicing the following methods, some people still will not be able to see the Aura. If you are such a person, do not worry about it. As I mentioned before, the ability to see the Aura is not required to perform successful Aura Healing.
- Relax, do not strain your eyes when trying to see the Aura and do not be concerned if you cannot see it the first few times you try.
- At the beginning, you might only be able to see the Aura for a few seconds, but in time it will appear for longer periods.
- Bright colored clothing should not be worn by either the person whose Aura you are trying to see or when trying to see your own Aura. If bright colors are worn, this will make seeing the Aura more of a challenge.

- The more you practice the following two methods, the odds of your success will increase.
- If after three minutes you do not see the Aura, stop the process and try again another day.

Technique One

1. Have a person stand in front of a white background or a solid, light-colored wall. Keep the lighting in the area to a minimum. (Illus. 67)

2. Stand about eight to ten feet in front of this person. (Illus. 68)

3. Take several steps to your left so you will not be facing the person directly. Now, pick a point a few inches over their left shoulder and focus on it for a few seconds. Next let your eyes relax while still looking at the point. (Illus. 69)

4. After several minutes you might be able to see some sort of haze, white glow, or colors around the person on their right side, that's the Aura. (Illus. 70)

5. Once you are able to see the Aura on one side of a person, move in front of them and focus your eyes on a point a few inches above their head for a few seconds. Then, let your eyes relax and you should be able to see the whole Aura. (Illus. 71)

Technique Two

1. Sit about three feet in front of a mirror. Keep the lighting in the area to a minimum and light reflection off the mirror. (Illus. 72)

2. Pick one shoulder and focus on a point a few inches over it for a few seconds. Next let your eyes relax while still looking at the point. (Illus. 73)

3. After a few minutes you might be able to see a white glow, a haze, or even colors around the side of the body opposite the point on which you focused. (Illus. 74)

4. Once you are able to see the Aura on one side of your body, focus on a point several inches over your head for a few seconds. Then, let your eyes relax and you should be able to see the whole Aura. (Illus. 75)

Illus. 67

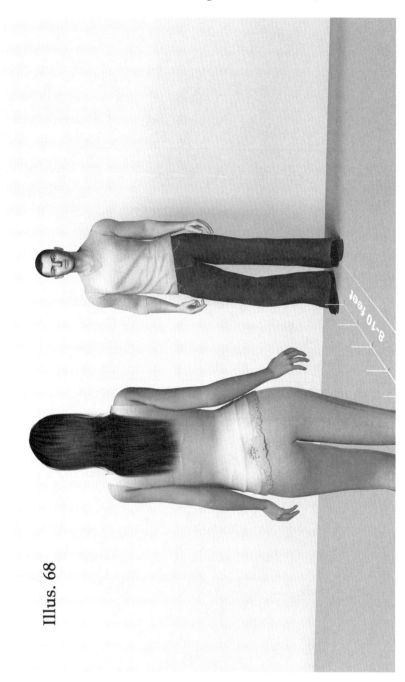

Illus. 68

8-10 feet

Illus. 69

185

Illus. 70

Illus. 71

Illus. 72

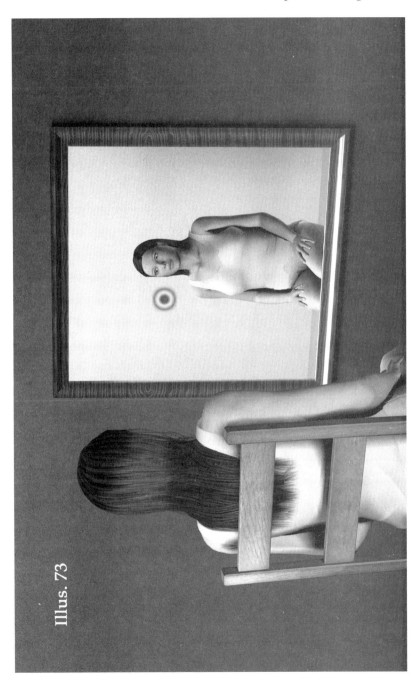

Illus. 73

Illus. 74

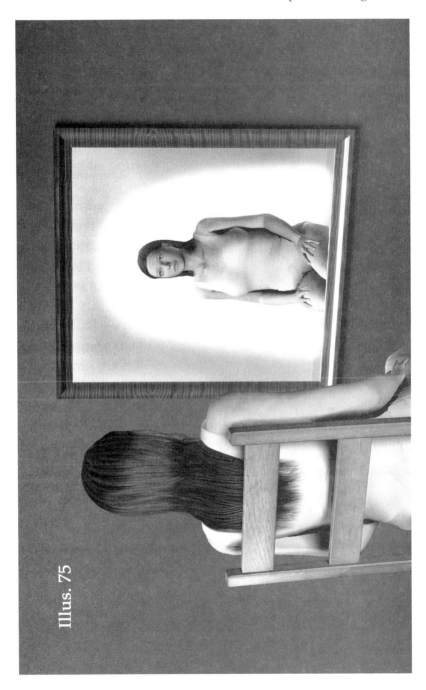

Illus. 75

191

There are a very few people select people who are not only able to see the Aura colors, but can also read and interpret them for illness and disease. Reading Aura colors for illness and disease is very subjective and I do not recommend doing this or even accepting a reading from a person who claims they can do this. Here is the reason why: The challenge with people who see Aura colors and diagnose them is that not all them perceive colors the same way. Color is determined in your brain via your eyes. For example, what I might perceive as purple, you might perceive as light red. This means you might have a healthy color in your Aura, but the person reading it will perceive it wrong and give you a wrong interpretation of the color.

Another difficulty is each person's Aura is individual and unique and so are their color combinations. A color described as "normal" for people in general in one book or chart could be an "abnormal" color for a few individuals. If you give out incorrect information in an Aura Reading for a disease or illness, even once, it can be harmful to the person receiving it.

It is my position that reading and interpreting Aura colors is not necessary if you become proficient in my method of Aura Healing because that is all you really will ever need for Aura Healing. Then you will never have to worry about giving incorrect information to a person about their state of health from Aura colors.

Words were never invented to fully explain the peaceful aura that surrounds us when we are in communion with minds of the same thoughts.

- Eddie Myers

The aura given out by a person or object is as much a part of them as their flesh.

- Lucian Freud

- Perform only one specific Aura Healing in a single session, then wait a minimum of three days before performing another.

- Since every person has different circumstances, the amount of Aura Healings needed for an issue will vary from person to person.

- If you or another person has multiple mental or emotional issues that need healing, perform the Aura Healing for the most pressing issue first. You can alternate the Aura Healing session every three days for the other issues.

- Change for the positive in the issue for which you received the Aura Healing might be instant or subtle at first. If subtle, as time progresses, you will have a more conscious awareness of the change.

- An Aura Healing removes Psychic Debris so the emotional or mental issue that created the debris can be resolved and/or released.

- Intent is the key factor in a successful Aura Healing. The Intent is determined by the emotional or mental issue that is causing problems in a person's life.

- You do not need to know if the issue for an Aura Healing is emotional or mental. The Aura Healing will remove all Psychic Debris stated in the Intent no matter if it originated in the Emotional Layer or the Mental Layer.

- If you look up definitions for mental and emotional issues, they either are related, or in some dictionaries, the definitions seem to be one and the same.

- Before performing an Aura Healing on yourself or another person, you must know the Intent for the Healing.

- Psychic Debris in the Emotional Layer always overlaps into the Mental Layer. Psychic Debris in the Mental Layer always overlaps into the Emotional Layer.

- People who can see Psychic Debris describe it as darkness spread throughout the first four layers of the Aura with most of the darkness in the Emotional and Mental Layers.

- What makes each Aura Healing different from another Aura Healing is the Intent used in the Healing.

- Once you become experienced performing an Aura Healing, it should never last longer than fifteen to thirty minutes.

- Aura Healing is only for emotional or mental issues. For physical ailments or diseases perform a Chakra Healing.

- After receiving an Aura Healing, your physical body may feel lighter because of the removal of Psychic Debris. This will only be temporary.

- You do not need to be exact when you visualize the spinning black hole. As long as it is about 14 to 16 inches away from the body, it will be in the Astral Layer.

- If there are multiple emotional or mental issues that require an Aura Healing, perform a Healing for one issue first, then wait a minimum of three days before performing one for a different issue.

- The Aura is much more than just a simple magnetic field surrounding your physical body; rather, it is a very complex system that is part of your very essence, which we have yet to fully understand.

- Your Aura and your physical body are the complete you, all one unit. You cannot have one without the other.

- Your Aura and your body communicate and exchange information that you need to exist and navigate in your physical life. This is done during every moment, awake or asleep, consciously or unconsciously.

- Our Auras contain the complete blueprints for our lives. Our consciousness and all our thoughts, feelings, and even awareness are integrated with and also stored in the Aura.

- The Aura contains all of our individual life moments until we die. These life experiences (memories) are carried forward and can reincarnated in future physical lives.

- The Aura reflects our health -- physically, mentally, emotionally, and spiritually. It also reflects our mental and emotional activity.

- The Aura is where a majority of mental and emotional issues can start. If these issues are not resolved, they eventually resonate down to the physical body and manifest as symptoms of an illness or a disease in the Chakras' Areas of Influence.

- The Aura can also show disease and ailments in the physical body before any symptoms have manifested there.

- One of the main sources of communication from the physical body to the Aura and the Aura back to the physical body are the Chakras.

He who has health, has hope; and he who
has hope, has everything

- Arabian Proverb

Aura Protection

16

Have you ever noticed yourself feeling tired or drained around some people? A person's Aura that is extremely out of balance and not healthy can drain your Aura's energy. The best protection for your Aura is to keep it balanced, healthy, and free of Psychic Debris. In this state it will naturally protect itself from energy drain from other person's unhealthy Aura.

I understand that your Aura might not be healthy on all occasions so you may need to protect your Aura at various times when you feel it is necessary. Protecting the Aura is not a natural occurrence. Ideally, Auras are healthy and interact and exchange information with other healthy Auras to help you with your life experience. You are not meant to walk around shielded from other Auras; but, unfortunately, the reality is we need to do so on various occasions to protect ourselves from an unhealthy Aura. There are several methods to protect your Aura when needed. They all will work. I prefer the following method when it is necessary to protect your Aura.

Protecting Your Aura

Visualize a protective shield or force field of white or golden light around your entire Aura about five feet out. Or, if you have difficulty with visualizing, just use your Intent and know or sense that it is in place. With this shield or force field in place, nothing can get in or out. What you can do is decide on a word (or words) that will instantly have it manifest in place and a word (or words) that will remove it. Keep this shield up until you are able to remove yourself from the interaction of the unhealthy Aura. Once this is done, remove the shield. Again, when Auras are healthy they are suppose to interact and exchange information to help with your life experience.

Index

A
Area of Influence 35
Astral Layer 116
Aura 14, 109, 110
Auric Layers 114
B
Back Chakras 21, 22, 26
Blocked Chakras 25
C
Celestial Layer 118
Chakra 13, 14, 31
Chi 18
E
Emotional Layer 116
Energy Bodies 114
Ether 116
Etheric Template Layer 118
I
Intent 54, 138, 139
K
Ketheric Layer 119
M
Mental Layer 117
Meridians 25, 26, 27
Minor Chakras 24
P
Psychic Debris 131, 132, 138
R
Reiki 18
S
Sage 55, 138
Secondary Chakras 24
Seven Major Chakras 19
Subtle Bodies 114
U
Universal Life Force 17, 18, 57
V
Visualize 54, 138

Bibliography

Pond, David. Chakras for Beginners: A Guide to Balancing Your Chakra Energies. Llewellyn Publications, 1999. ISBN-13: 978-1567185379

Anodea Judith, Wheels of Life: A User's Guide to the Chakra System. Llewellyn Publications, 1987. ISBN-13: 978-0875423203

Mercier, Patricia. The Chakra Bible: The Definitive Guide to Chakra Energy. Sterling, 2007. ISBN-13: 978-1402752247.

Saradananda, Swami. Chakra Meditation: Discover Energy, Creativity, Focus, Love, Communication, Wisdom, and Spirit. Duncan Baird, 2008. ISBN-13: 978-1844834952

Wauters, Ambika. The Book of Chakras: Discover the Hidden Forces Within. Barron, 2002. ISBN-13: 978-0764121074

Davies, Brenda. The 7 Healing Chakras: Unlocking Your Body's Energy Centers. Ulysses Press, 2000. ISBN-13: 978-1569751688

Andrews, Ted. How To See and Read The Aura. Llewellyn Publications, 2006. ISBN-13: 978-0738708157

Smith, Mark. Auras: See Them in Only 60 seconds. Llewellyn Publications, 2002. ISBN-13: 978-1567186437

Cayce, Edgar. Auras: An Essay on the Meaning of Colors. A.R.E. Press, 1973. ISBN-13: 978-0876040126

Webster, Richard. Aura Reading for Beginners: Develop Your Psychic Awareness. Llewellyn Publications, 2002. ISBN-13: 978-1567187984

Kul, Kurhum and Kul Djwal. The Human Aura: How to Achieve and Energize Your Aura and Chakras. Summit University Press,1996. ISBN-13: 978-0922729258

More of what people are saying...

I stumbled upon Reiki The Ultimate Guide. It was as if I was guided by an instance! After skimming through reviews, I immediately took a chance. I can honestly now say, "This book is Great!" Good straight to the point answers and the words just flow with ease. This is honestly a Very Good Reiki reference book to have! I have now found a good author and Reiki teacher to learn from and am looking forward to more books and dvds in the future! *C.G.*

As fellow traveler, I recommend Steve Murray's series of Reiki Books, CDs, and DVDs. After having explored both the in person attunements and the distance attunements, the only difference was price and secrecy. Now, as a Master, after five years of study, the only materials I find worth referencing or quoting, are those of Steve Murray's. He has taken an archaic subject and simplified it into easy one, two, three steps. There are no frills, no hidden agenda, and no need for secrecy, just the unadorned truth of the subject. You could explore other Reiki courses, but you will not find a more complete, comprehensible and affordable program anywhere on the web. The only thing you get with Mr. Murray is the quickest and fastest way to learn and experience the Healing Art of Reiki. Thank you, Mr. Murray, Thank you. *N.D.H.*

Before finding Steve I was a Reiki II Practitioner and spent $300 on that training. I was seriously considering paying the $500 to become a Reiki Master when I came upon Steve's DVDs. I am now a Reiki Master through Steve's Reiki Master DVD and have recently begun teaching Reiki Classes. It's been one of the most amazing experiences of my life. I have a master's degree in education and am a former schoolteacher and absolutely LOVE Steve's work and his simple, straightforward presentation style. My students love his books and the DVDs provide excellent reinforcement in the classes I teach. *J.G.*

It takes awhile to read all of these books and view the DVDs, which I view constantly. They are incredible. I must tell you that there is no one else that I believe in as much as I do you to have as my Reiki Master Instructor. You are totally on target in your books and on your DVDs. *B.E.*

I haven't even finished reading the book, but I did page through until the end. The chakra locations for many animals in itself is priceless. The pictures showing chakra locations and how to do balancing, etc. is also great. Wonderful book as I am looking to continue my current Reiki healing of animals. This is a fantastic "how to" that is easy to understand and follow. *D.C.*

After being trained in the Usui system of Reiki and practicing it for about 7 years, Steve Murray has provided me with a fuller training experience. He has expanded the Usui oral tradition into the written word & beautiful video & audio experiences. Steve's books and DVDs filled the gap in my ongoing Reiki training. I highly recommend them. *R.B.*

Of course I was very skeptical about getting the attunement by a DVD and thought 'how in the world can you receive the attunement by a DVD? But alas, I do feel the energy in my palms strongly and when I intend to use Reiki. Now, I believe that the attunement can be received using the DVD. I will have the 2nd level attunement with his DVD! *K.H.*

I purchased all 7 volumes of Steve Murrays books and all of his DVDs. I'm here to tell you, it was one of the best investments I have ever made!! From the time I opened the first Ultimate Guide, answers came faster than I could have ever imagined. Through the straightforward and concise information in these materials, I have a renewed confidence. With the first book, I have learned more in one sitting than I had in several years of questioning. A special thank you goes to Steve Murray for his outstanding work. *K.M.*

Information on Chakra/Aura Healer Certification

Also available are two DVDs by Steve Murray: Aura Healing Step by Step and Chakra Healing Step by Step which show Steve performing Aura and Chakra Healing sessions on camera. Both DVDs complement the book and are great study tools. In fact since you already own the book, if you acquire both DVDs, Steve will certify you as a Chakra/Aura Healer. Information on the Chakra/Aura Healer certification program on his website: www.healingreiki.com or email bodymindheal@aol.com

About the Author

Steve Murray is the author of the global best-selling Reiki the Ultimate Guide books and has over 45 self-help programs on DVD. A few examples of the topics on DVD are: Reiki Healing, Psychic Healing, Soul Retrieval, Aura and Chakra Healing, Removing Psychic Debris, Contacting Angels, Past Life Healing, Cancer Imagery, Weight Loss, and Pain, Fear, and Stress Relief.